The Battle of
Bellicourt Tunnel

The Battle of Bellicourt Tunnel

Tommies, Diggers and Doughboys
on the Hindenburg Line, 1918

Dale Blair

Foreword by
Gary Sheffield

Frontline Books, London

The Battle of Bellicourt Tunnel:
Tommies, Diggers and Doughboys on the Hindenburg Line, 1918

This edition published in 2011 by Frontline Books,
an imprint of
Pen & Sword Books Limited,
47 Church Street, Barnsley, S. Yorkshire, S70 2AS
www.frontline-books.com

Email info@frontline-books.com or write to us at the above address.

ISBN: 978-1-84832-587-6

CIP data records for this title are available from the British Library

Designed and typeset by Wordsense Ltd, Edinburgh in Bembo 11/16pt

Printed in Great Britain by CPI Antony Rowe

Contents

Illustrations

Maps

Abbreviations

AEF   American Expeditionary Force

AIF   Australian Imperial Force

AWM   Australian War Memorial

BEF   British Expeditionary Force

GSO1   general staff officer (grade 1)

IWM   Imperial War Museum

NCO   Non-commissioned officer

RFA   Royal Field Artillery

US-MO   *United States Army in the World War 1917–1919, Military Operations of the American Expeditionary Forces, Somme Offensive*, vol. 7

Foreword

From August to November 1918 the British Expeditionary Force (BEF) under Field-Marshal Sir Douglas Haig fought a series of victorious battles on the Western Front that contributed mightily to the defeat of the Imperial German Army. It did so as part of a coalition, and the role of French, Belgian and United States forces should not be forgotten. The BEF itself, it is often forgotten, was a coalition force. While troops from the British Isles provided the core, the four divisions of the Canadian Corps, the five division-strong Australian Corps, the New Zealand Division (by 1918 standards the size of a small corps) and the South African Brigade were powerful accretions of strength. Such formations were both part of the BEF and proto-national armies in their own right. Many, probably most, Dominion soldiers had no difficulty in regarding themselves as both Australians (or whatever) and in some sense 'British'. In September 1918 General Sir Henry Rawlinson's British Fourth Army had a further level of coalition complexity with which to cope. The American II Corps was placed under the tutelage of Lieutenant-General Sir John Monash's Australian Corps. Thus the attack on the Bellicourt Tunnel, the subject of Dale Blair's book, was very much an inter-Allied affair.

Dale Blair is a fine historian who has already written, among other things, *Dinkum Diggers,* a path-breaking study of the Australian Imperial Force's 1st Battalion. Here he employs a similar forensic approach, giving detailed description and incisive analysis of the operations of the Australian and American II Corps in the Hindenburg Line fighting. British readers who have more than a passing knowledge in the 'Hundred Days' will be familiar with the feats of 46th (North Midland) Division a short distance down the canal: 137 (Staffordshire) Brigade succeeded in forcing a crossing and thereby unlocking the German defences. What happened on the flank, in the Australian/American sector, is much less well known, and Dale Blair's achievement is to tell a complicated story in a highly readable fashion.

Dr Blair's judgements are uncompromising. He, fairly, points the finger of blame at Haig, Rawlinson and Monash for expecting too much of the raw American troops, singling out the Australian Corps commander for particular criticism. Up against a tough enemy protected by formidable defences, neither the inexperienced Americans nor the battle-hardened diggers could be expected to prevail easily. A technological quick fix was not the answer: the battle of 29 September was, he judges, correctly, 'disastrous' for the Tank Corps. Overall, the fighting in the Tunnel sector was, he argues persuasively, a draw. At the end, like two boxers, the Australian–American force was gasping for breath and the Germans, badly battered, were back-pedalling to remain on balance. This is a fair conclusion for this stretch of front, but overall the day was calamitous for the German Army, even if the clean breakthrough that Haig had hoped for did not occur. Forced out of the Hindenburg Line, the prognosis for the German Army on the Western Front – and hence Imperial Germany itself – was bleak indeed.

Dale Blair has written a book that stands as a distinguished contribution to the military history of the First World War. This detailed study of an important battle adds significantly to our understanding of a critical phase in the fighting. No one writing about or teaching the history of the final offensives of 1918 can afford to ignore it.

Gary Sheffield
Professor of War Studies, University of Birmingham

Acknowledgements

The writing of this book was partly assisted through the award of an Australian Army History Unit research grant in 2004. This grant allowed me the luxury of travelling overseas to walk the battlefield and to visit archives in the UK.

While in France I was the recipient of wonderful hospitality from long-time friends Claude and Colette Durand and their family. In England, too, I was treated royally by Jenny Stephens and her brother Jeremy while staying in London.

My thanks to Gary Sheffield, who on short notice was able to gain me necessary clearance to access archival records at King's College and the Imperial War Museum. He has also kindly provided the foreword to this book for which I am grateful.

Mitch Yockelson was particularly helpful in clarifying some aspects of the American involvement in the battle and sharing information.

The book has lain dormant for nearly three years due to unfulfilled promises in Australia so it is with great relief and much appreciation that I acknowledge the enthusiasm for the project by Michael Leventhal at Frontline Books.

My heartfelt thanks to my wife, Non, who, as always, has steered me through the vagaries of the computer while completing the manuscript and who suffered, relatively silently, the long period over which the 1:10,000 map of the battlefield carpeted the rumpus room floor.

Introduction

After the cessation of hostilities in the First World War, Lieutenant-General Sir John Monash reflected on the actions of his Australian Corps in his book *The Australian Victories in France in 1918*. He noted that his Corps, numbering nearly 200,000 men as it prepared for the breakthrough battle against the Hindenburg Line, was four times as large as the British Army under the command of the Duke of Wellington at Waterloo.[1] It is likely that the Iron Duke and other Napoleonic generals would have found the nature of warfare so changed by mechanical and technical progress as to be inconceivable to their early nineteenth-century sensibilities. Even more so if consideration was given to the fact that Monash's expanded corps represented only seven of sixty-two divisions making up five British armies stretching from the Channel ports to the Somme river.

Apart from the myriad ancillary troops attached to the Australian Corps at this time by far the most significant component accounting for its large size was the attachment of the American II Corps of two divisions, the 27th (New York) Division and the 30th (Tennessee/North Carolina) Division. This corps had been assigned to Monash to bolster the depleted stocks of his homegrown troops in preparation for another attempted breakthrough battle. At that time, the attrition of four years of war was biting deeply into the Australian ranks. The massive battles of 1917 had inflicted a third of the total casualties suffered by the Australians in all theatres of war during the 1914–18 conflict. Although the soldiers had voted in favour of conscription in two referenda, the Australian nation as a whole had voted against the proposition. With no obvious well of reinforcements to draw on, the Australian Imperial Force (AIF) was forced to rely on a diminishing pool of volunteers and a trickle of returning convalescents.

In the Battle of the Hindenburg outpost line (which preceded the Bellicourt Tunnel operation) the Australian 1st Division could count just short of three thousand rifles and the Australian 4th Division only marginally more. This was well under a third of the recommended strength of a British division. By Monash's estimation, these two divisions were spent and needed to be rested if they were to be available for the seemingly inevitable spring campaign in 1919.

It was while Monash was putting forward his case for their replenishment that his commanding officer, the Fourth Army's Lieutenant-General Sir Henry Rawlinson, asked if his Australian subordinate might continue operations if supplied with fresh reinforcements. The American 27th and 30th Divisions had become available for British use in mid-August after the American commander, General John Pershing, had agreed to allow them to remain with the British Army provided they were retained under command of their own officers while the other American divisions then training with the British were withdrawn. This was a marked departure from his earlier insistence that all American troops were to form part of a larger independent US Army. Monash, who had been impressed with the enthusiasm and metal of the Americans during the Hamel battle in July, was more than happy to accept this offer if it could be arranged.

During the battles of May/June/July American troops had been thrown into the fray as reinforcements for the French and British armies. They had acquitted themselves admirably and the hundreds of thousands of American troops arriving in France on a monthly basis were a godsend to the French and British armies, which had been bled white from the recent offensives and accumulated effects of four years of war. Training of the newly arriving American troops and acclimatising them to front-line conditions began in earnest.

Although the American declaration of war had occurred on 6 April 1917, it had taken twelve months for the American mobilisation to allow sufficient numbers of doughboys to arrive in Europe to bolster the Allied armies. The American Expeditionary Force (AEF) arrived with men and small arms. Apart from the uniform on their back they relied mainly on the British Army for the supply of tanks, 'limbers, water carts, officer's mess carts, rolling kitchens, harnesses, animals, ordnance . . . gas masks and steel helmets. Cartridge belts and bayonets were collected and replaced with British Lee Enfields, British belts and British bayonets.'[2] French planes and artillery were also provided.

Agreement for the training of American troops under British command had been formalised on 12 February 1918 and was to follow a three-step process.[3] This entailed the attachment of American platoons to larger formations, then companies, eventuating in the placement of whole larger American formations in the front line with independent command authority. In June the British commander-in-chief, Haig, made a request to Pershing for American troops to be used in a defensive role in the event of an emergency. The American 27th and 33rd Divisions, and later the 30th, 78th and 80th Divisions, were moved closer to the front near Amiens to fulfil that need if required.[4]

The German 1918 spring offensive launched on 21 March had threatened to unhinge the Allied war effort when it ruptured the British lines. Four to six weeks elapsed before the Allies began to stabilise their broken front. During this crisis the Australians played a notable part in plugging the gaps and holding the line with four divisions operating in the Somme region and a fifth, the 1st Division, sent to the Strazeele and Meteren sector further north.

The operation in which Monash and his expanded corps were about to enter had evolved from the general successes gained by the British Army since its line had been shattered by the German spring offensive. By mid-May it was obvious the German Army had failed in its attempts to break the British line. The questionable decision by General Ludendorff to break off the push in the north, in favour of a new strike further south against the French, allowed the British the respite they needed to reorganise and replenish.

During this crisis, the magnitude of the impending disaster being the most acute since the Battle of the Marne in 1914, Haig found himself very much the man of the hour. It is doubtful that a better officer existed in the army at that moment in time possessing the necessary resolve to take on the weighty burden that was then thrust on his shoulders. Haig, much criticised by contemporaries and historians for a lack of imagination both strategically and tactically, was ever the optimist. He also had an unshakeable belief in the quality of the British soldiers and of the righteousness of the cause for which they fought. He was dour and, in the best traditions of stereotypical British character, endowed with a great stubbornness and fighting spirit. This attitude was clearly communicated to his troops in his famous 'backs to the wall' entreaty during the potentially catastrophic events of the early spring.

Throughout his generalship, Haig had been an ardent believer in the value of offensive action. His critics have argued that he was blind to tactical and strategic realities as a result and that he wasted lives in pushing on when it was obvious that the offensive had broken down and a breakthrough unachievable. Passchendaele or the Third Ypres campaign is often cited as an example of this. Whether true or not, the time had now arrived where the long sought-after breakthrough battle of Haig's imagination might just be possible. The arrival of large numbers of American troops at the front during May and June coupled with the sensible decision, made during the height of the German offensive, to appoint a supreme allied commander-in-chief all promised concerted and decisive action in the summer to come.

The mantle of Supreme Allied commander was bestowed on General Foch in the Hotel de Ville at Doullens on 26 March during a meeting of British and French generals. The immediate overriding concern for Foch and all his generals was to withstand the German attacks and hold a secure line. One of the first initiatives undertaken by Foch was to dispatch nine French divisions to act as a reserve to the British armies, though Haig thought they had been tardily offered and then not committed in full. Although the British Fifth Army had been smashed and rendered ineffective in the initial shock of the March battles, the British line was re-established albeit having to concede much of the ground won over the previous two years.

Further north, where Ludendorff struck his second blow, the Australian 1st Division did good work around Hazebrouck where it blunted the German advance and contributed to the prevention of a German breakthrough to the Channel ports. Australian soldiers were keenly aware of the dire circumstances that faced the British armies at that point in time and many saw themselves, in this moment of crisis, as being Britain's last hope.

By the end of April the British line had been consolidated and Ludendorff switched his main attention to the southwest, looking desperately for a way through the French defences. The Aisne offensive, Ludendorff's third major attack, was launched on 27 May and succeeded in penetrating to a maximum depth of twenty miles before eventually being contained. A fourth attempt was made in June in the Noyon–Montdidier sector. This was quickly stifled by a forewarned French command and a fifth offensive, launched in mid-July against the Champagne–Marne sector achieved only limited success.

The stage was now set for Foch to assume offensive operations. On the British front it was the Australians under Monash who delivered one of the first decisive counterblows at Hamel on 4 July. The undertaking of the attack on American Independence Day was no accident. It had been selected to honour the ten companies of Americans that had been assigned to the Australian 4th Division for the action. On the eve of the stunt the ten were reduced to four following objections from General Pershing who was of the opinion that their use contravened the agreement to use American troops only if a critical situation arose.[5]

Although only a two-brigade attack, Hamel was important for a number of reasons. It heralded the introduction of the new Mark V tanks, the success of which went a long way to restoring Australian confidence in the tanks after their calamitous failure at Bullecourt a year earlier. This acceptance of the improved operational capacity of the tanks was a crucial step for their widespread employment in later battles. Of equal if not greater significance was the improvement in sound-ranging techniques by the artillery to pinpoint the location of the enemy batteries. This allowed for the neutralisation of the German guns in the preliminary bombardment giving the infantry and tanks the benefit of a less taxing advance. A further element was the fostering of mutual respect between Australian and American troops. For many doughboys the Australians were a refreshing tonic to the generally negative American view of the British, which seems to have prevailed in the training phase. Australian suspicions of the newcomers were also broken down with direct contact although the Bellicourt Tunnel action would throw up new challenges as to how that relationship would be interpreted.

Both prior to and after the Hamel fight Australian patrolling had been vigorous and aggressive and saw large sections of the German line seized in a process that became known euphemistically as peaceful penetration. These small-scale operations pushed the Germans back along the width of the Australian front and aided the seizure of suitable ground from which to launch a counteroffensive to quash the German salient at Amiens.

The first stage of Foch's plan was to eradicate the German salient formed as a result of their earlier attacks. A counteroffensive known as the Second Battle of the Marne began on 18 July and marked the beginning of what became known as the Hundred Day campaign. After two weeks' fighting the Germans were pushed out of the salient back to the line of the Aisne and Velse rivers. Foch was rewarded with a promotion to Marshal of France by a buoyant Georges Clemenceau – the French prime minister – but the most important upshot of the success was that Ludendorff's plans for a renewal of the offensive against the British in Flanders

MAP I *Foch's planned series of blows against the Germans*

were shelved, signifying that the pendulum of opportunity had swung back in favour of the Allies. The Amiens salient was Foch's next target.

The Amiens offensive was launched on 8 August or '*der scharwze Tag*' as Ludendorff would famously dub it. The Australians and Canadians spearheaded an impressive breakthrough that drove the Germans back nine miles and succeeded in Foch's aim of eliminating the German salient. It was the first time that all five Australian infantry divisions had fought as one corps despite the Australian Corps' creation in November 1917, to which Monash was appointed commander in May 1918.

Following the success at Amiens Haig widened his attack. Sir Julian Byng's Third Army attacked northwest of Bapaume and made a gain of three miles. Under Haig's urging Byng pressed on and forced the Germans back further. Haig switched back to the Fourth Army front. North of the Somme Albert was captured and south of the river Herleville was obtained, thus opening the way to St Quentin. The Australians were again prominent.

The Australians had been continuously in the line since April. Grumbling and dissatisfaction among the men were much in evidence by mid-September. Some diggers thought the Australians were being asked to do more than their fair share. In truth, the British divisions with which the Australians drew so many invidious distinctions had as much cause for complaint. Monash knew his men were weary but he believed in the Napoleonic maxim of feeding the troops on victory and to achieve that success the Australian commander adhered to the Stonewall Jacksonian style of driving the men beyond their perceived limits of endurance. The crowning success of this philosophy came with the impressive capture of Mont St Quentin and Peronne in the three days between 29 August and 1 September in what was perhaps the finest feat of Australian arms during the course of the war. The German hold on the Somme river defences was rendered untenable as a result and it was a matter of prudent necessity that they take up a new defensive line. Equally impressive was the Canadian Corp's rupture of the Drocourt–Queant switch in the Arras sector. Attached to General Sir Henry Horne's First Army their success forced the Germans back into an emergency line in front of Cambrai.

South of Verdun the third German salient at St Mihiel was attacked by Pershing's US Army on 12 September. The Germans were in the process of evacuating the salient when the American assault fell on them and they lost some 15,000 prisoners. With the third salient reduced the stage was now set for Foch's grand attack on Germany's great fortress – the Hindenburg Line as it was best known to the Allies.

On the British Fourth Army front a preliminary attack was needed to bring the line into position for the main assault. This commenced on 18 September and was known generally as the battle for the Hindenburg outpost line. Its undertaking had been hastened forward following the successful capture of Havrincourt on 12 September by Byng's Third Army. The advance pushed the line forward three miles, the Australian 1st and 4th Divisions being particularly successful in the centre. A critical failure was the inability of the British III Corps to take the ground on its front. This would have dire consequences for the proposed main attack.

From the Australian perspective, the Hindenburg outpost line proved to be the last battle of the Australian 1st and 4th Divisions. The numeric deficiencies of these divisions had been a major concern for Monash in the planning of the outpost line battle. Exacerbating his concerns was the fact that only eight tanks were available for the attack. The losses and breakdowns sustained in the August counteroffensive had necessitated a complete overhaul and refitting of this valuable arm of service, which Monash had integrated so successfully in his tactics at Hamel and Amiens. To compensate for this loss of protection and the depleted numbers of infantry, Monash doubled the number of machine guns in the divisions by attaching the machine-gun battalions of the 3rd and 5th Divisions. This echoed the tactic, already introduced, of increasing the number of Lewis guns in the front line to increase firepower. On 18 September, 1,500 artillery provided a creeping barrage while 256 Vickers machine guns delivered an intense and terrifying barrage in support of the infantry along the 7,000-yard front that cowed the German defenders and was a significant factor in the success of the operation. One German battalion officer who experienced the barrage commented to his captors, 'The small-arms fire was too terrible for words. There was nothing to be done but to crouch down in our trenches and wait for you to come and take us.'[6] The success of this operation placed the British within striking distance of the main German defences.

On 26 September 1918 the first of four great hammer blows fell on the German Army. Foch hoped that these attacks delivered in quick succession would destabilise the German front and penetrate through to the vital rail junctions behind the German lines, the capture of which would jeopardise Germany's capacity to supply its armies. In the south French and American troops attacked between the Meuse and Rheims. The next day the British First Army and some of the Third struck at Cambrai. In Flanders, on 28 September, French, Belgian and British armies combined to deliver a third strike. All made immediate significant gains. The final anticipated knockout punch was to be delivered by Rawlinson's Fourth Army on 29 September – a Sunday.

CHAPTER ONE

The Plan

_____

'There can be no question of going back a single step further.'
– General Ludendorff

On the afternoon of 13 September General Rawlinson, commander of the British Fourth Army, called his corps commanders together at Assevillers for an informal discussion about the course of forthcoming operations against the Hindenburg Line. There, in the newly hutted headquarters camp of Lieutenant-General John Monash's Australian Corps, Lieutenant-General Sir R. Butler (III Corps), Lieutenant-General Sir W. Braithwaite (IX Corps), the Australian general and army commander met over a cup of tea to give thought to the task at hand.

The generals were buoyed by their possession of detailed plans captured during the 8 August battle of the section of the German defence scheme south of Bellicourt. These papers had been captured by the crew of an armoured car from the 17th Battalion Tank Corps from a German HQ in the village of Framerville. The captured plans detailed every searchlight, machine-gun pit, observation post, telephone exchange, command station, gun and mortar emplacement. As well, they were appended with notes about the tactical strengths of all topographical features within the system. Although the scheme had been devised the previous year and even with knowledge that these important papers had been lost to the enemy, there was little room for significant change on the part of the Germans to the guiding principles that underpinned the plan.[1]

1

Rawlinson and his generals agreed on a two-stage operation. It was realised that the depth and strength of the enemy's position would be impossible to overrun in a single day. The concentration of German divisions in this part of the front was much denser than any other sector. The first phase would constitute the capture of the Hindenburg outpost line, which lay east of the old British front line lost in the March offensive. With its capture the jumping-off point for the second stage, the attack on the main German line, would be attained.

The attack on the outpost line began on 18 September. The Fourth Army front stretched from opposite the village of Vendhuille on the St Quentin Canal down to the historic town of St Quentin on the Somme river. The III Corps formed the left or northern part of the army front, the Australian Corps the centre and IX Corps the right or southern portion. The attack proved a resounding success in the centre and on the right but on the left III Corps struggled to make the ground allotted to them. The section of the line they were attacking lay squarely opposite the Bellicourt Tunnel sector.

The tunnel constituted a 6,256-yard underground section of the continuous waterway that connected the cities of Cambrai and St Quentin. A towpath ran along the entire eastern edge of the canal. Completed by Napoleon's engineers in 1812 the canal went by a number of names. From Cambrai to Le Catelet it was known as the Canal de l'Escaut; from Le Catelet to Bellicourt it was called the Canal Souterrain; and from Riquevel to St Quentin it was the Canal de St Quentin. The main tunnel was called the Bellicourt Tunnel. Its northern entrant was located at Vendhuille and ran in a straight line on a southerly axis underneath the town of Bellicourt to its southern entrant above Bellenglise near Riqueval.[2]

The tunnel itself was however of limited defensive value. Rather, it was the high ground west of it that would cause the most heartache to the attacking British, American and Australian soldiers. This area was particularly well defended and the failure to crack this defensive nut was to play with dire effect on subsequent operations. Whereas the German canal defences south of the tunnel were graced by the obvious benefits of a waterway dominated by 50- to 60-foot bluffs and steep embankments, the tunnel sector offered a natural bridge through the German line. A spoil of dirt about ten yards in width ran along the top of the tunnelled sector and was laced with machine-gun posts with many – but not all – entrants running down to the tunnel itself. This line was referred to as the tunnel mound. Anti-tank guns were also concentrated through this area as it was the obvious sector in which tanks could be used. To compensate further for the perceived weakness of the tunnel position, the German planners erected heavy belts of barbed wire in front of both their main line and their outpost line. These were five deep in places and were characterised by the thickness in which they were massed. The main Hindenburg Line behind the wire was made up of two broad and deep trench lines with interlocking communication trenches and approach lanes. The section of this line facing the British Fourth Army was known as the Siegfried Stellung (position) to the Germans. Two extra defence systems were constructed behind the main line known as Le Catelet–Nauroy Line and the Beaurevoir Line, the latter being somewhat less developed than the others.

The most significant spoiling tactic employed by the Germans was to occupy the high ground west of the tunnel sector. Here three positions dominated the landscape. They were, from north to south, the Knoll, Gillemont Farm and Quennemont Farm. The occupation of this high ground and the buildings thereon allowed the Germans to keep the British artillery at a reasonably safe distance from their main line. Moreover, the long sweeping gradations that needed to be traversed to approach them meant that advancing infantry without sufficient artillery support would be subject to a deadly fire from well-sited machine guns. The German's stated intention in 1917 was to defend the outpost line for as long as possible and to abandon it if attacked by 'considerable forces'.[3] They would then rely on defending the area in depth via Le Catelet–Nauroy and Beaurevoir lines.

In September 1918 the Hindenburg Line had assumed far greater importance than its tactical and strategic meaning to the armies that defended it. It was the most tangible and singular bargaining chip available to German diplomats seeking peace proposals. As Ludendorff stated:

> There can be no question of going back a single step further. We must show the British, French, and Americans that any further attacks on the Siegfried Line will be utterly broken, and that that line is an impregnable rampart, with the result that the Entente Powers will condescend to consider the terms of peace which it is absolutely necessary for us to have before we can end the war.[4]

Although Rawlinson's sounding out of Monash for the use of the Americans was made prior to the conclusion of the outpost line operation, confirmation did not come until later. Major-General G. W. Read's II Corps comprising the 27th and 30th Divisions was attached to Monash's Australian Corps. Read was a regular officer of the US Army. Born thirteen days after Abraham Lincoln's election in 1860 his two divisions were state guard units.

Monash first met with Read on 20 September to discuss the necessary arrangements for the attachment. For the forthcoming operation Read sensibly ceded battlefield control of his divisions to Monash. The American general well understood the complications that an extra tier of command might add to the conduct of the forthcoming battle. The short suite in the American hand was their obvious lack of battlefield experience. Monash hoped to circumvent this weakness through meticulous planning and instruction of the American senior and junior officers. To facilitate the integration and planning of the Americans, Monash formed an Australian mission of line officers and non-commissioned officers (NCOs) drawn from the Australian 1st and 4th Divisions. These were the two Australian divisions that the Americans were replacing.

By contrast with the dwindling numbers in the Australian divisions the American II Corps numbered nearly 50,000 men, their standard division

4

strength being double the British model. They would be a welcome addition. Thus Monash's fighting command, on the eve of the battle, would comprise the two American divisions, the Australian 2nd, 3rd and 5th Divisions with the 5 Cavalry Brigade detached from the 2nd Cavalry Division in reserve plus artillery and corps ancillary troops.[5]

The attachment of the American II Corps was part of a general replenishment and freshening of Rawlinson's Fourth Army. During the August battles its fourteen divisions had suffered 50,000 casualties. The men were tired but optimistic. It was evident to even the most hardened cynic that real gains were beginning to be made against the Germans. If the pressure was to be maintained new troops were needed. The British 1st Division, which had been spared major fighting since the Passchendaele battle the previous year, was transferred from Horne's First Army. The 6th Division which had not launched a major assault since the Cambrai offensive in November 1917 was also added as was the 46th North Midland Division from Fifth Army. Their last battle had been Hill 70 in August 1917 with the First Army. These divisions, along with the 32nd Division, were formed into a reconstituted IX Corps.[6]

Troops were brought from Italy and Macedonia, where they had been unscarred by heavy fighting in the past twelve months, and added to the 25th and 50th Divisions. The 66th East Lancashire Division was also restocked with Lancastrians, Irishmen and South Africans from other theatres. The 58th London Division and 74th Division were sent to quieter sectors. The new divisions were attached to XIII Corps headquarters and became the army reserve.[7]

When Rawlinson had secured Monash's agreement to attach the Americans to his command and attack the Hindenburg Line he asked the Australian to draw up a preliminary plan of operations. This request was probably made in the meeting with his corps commanders on 13 September. By 18 September, in the midst of the outpost line operations, Monash had managed to conceive a remarkably detailed and coherent battle plan for Rawlinson's consideration. Monash's capacity for such planning was, in part, a legacy of his civil engineering background. It was also honed by the studious attention he applied to the logistical element of command practised in his prewar militia days coupled with his study of previous military campaigns. One key plank of the plan was that it assumed the Hindenburg outpost line would be fully in British possession by the date of attack.[8]

The battlefield map of operations designated three distinct lines around which the timetables and movements would be arranged. The Brown Line was the start line. It was drawn on the old Hindenburg outpost line. The Green Line, which was the American and British objective, ran from Vendhuille in the north, through Le Catelet and Guoy and down the eastern face of Le Catelet Line to Nauroy and back to the canal bank above Bellenglise in the south. The Red Line was the Beurevoir–Fonsomme Line.

Monash's intention was to push the two American divisions forward over the tunnel position to the Green Line. Once this was reached the Americans would consolidate their position while the Australian 3rd and 5th Divisions passed through. Cavalry and tanks would then join the assaulting Australian divisions, which could then attempt to take the Red Line behind the main Hindenburg defences. This drive would of course leave the Australian and American flanks exposed. To protect them Monash proposed that the IX Corps could follow behind and turn southward on the right flank to take the German canal defenders from behind thus eliminating any costly assault across the canal itself. The III Corps would undertake a similar movement on the left flank.

Rawlinson called his commanders together again at Monash's headquarters on the 19 September to lay before them his plan of battle. In relation to the Australian general's proposal the army commander made two significant alterations. The first was that the IX Corps was asked to assault the German defences frontally across the canal. Monash had considered this an ill-advised and costly tactic, one that he said he would not have asked of his own troops and one that he could not, in good conscience, propose for others not under

6

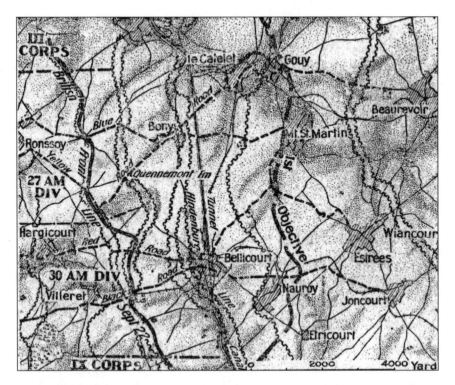

MAP 2 *Intended first objective (Green Line) of the Fourth Army attack showing Blue, Yellow, Red and Black roads*

his command. Rawlinson's decision to commit the IX Corps to this attack was possibly influenced by Foch's plan, only just announced, to make a combined assault by four armies on the German line. The assumption was that the broader the front the less likelihood there would be of German reserves being used to bolster defenders at the breakthrough points. It was sound logic that worked as well on the smaller tactical level as it did on the grand tactical or strategic levels. Co-ordination of all parts would be the vital key to success. The III Corps was to be replaced by the XIII Corps on the left and it was to follow through the breach, if the Australians and Americans were successful, and turn north to envelope the German positions. The second significant alteration was

7

that the Beaurevoir Line was not to be set as an objective for the first day of operations. Its capture was an ambitious concept but one that Rawlinson felt would be better considered after the condition and success of the troops could be assessed on first reaching the initial objectives.

Official orders for the Fourth Army operation were issued on 22 September. The main attack was scheduled for Sunday 29 September. The Brown Line was at that stage a proposed line only as some of the ground it included had yet to be won. This ground was that directly opposite the tunnel sector, which the III Corps had been unable to secure in the outpost line operation. As the III Corps was to be replaced by the XIII Corps and as that corps was designated a position further to the left, the capture of this ground was left to the Americans. Haig, alert to the lessons of past battles, preferred that the inexperienced Americans be preserved for the main attack and not worn out in a potentially exhausting preliminary fight. Rawlinson was able to persuade Haig otherwise, citing the exhaustion and his dissatisfaction with the III Corps' performance as his principal reasons.

The American objective in the main operation was delineated by the Green Line. It encompassed the capture of Le Catelet–Nauroy Line and a couple of hundred yards beyond. At its furthest point it lay 4,000 yards from the start line. When added to the 1,000 yards that the Americans needed to reach their jump-off position then one can begin to appreciate the enormity of the task they were being set. No Australian troops had ever been asked to advance 5,000 yards to an objective in a single action. It was a huge task to set for unseasoned troops and commanders. The Australian objective beyond the Beaurevoir Line was not, under Rawlinson's plan, expected to be reached on the first day. Requiring an advance over open ground with minimal artillery support this was a phase that would need great skill on the part of the troops undertaking it.

As usual with a set-piece battle a preliminary bombardment would be brought down on the enemy. The Fourth Army artillery had 1,634 guns and howitzers available to pummel the German defenders in a four-day barrage.[9]

This represented a concentration of one gun per three yards. Given the knowledge gleaned from captured documents and the improved range-finding methods used by the British artillery, this phase of the operation was expected to prove devastatingly effective. Adding to this compelling belief was the fact that the British barrage would include the use of mustard gas for the first time. Fifty thousand mustard gas shells were delivered to the Fourth Army front. Having been victims of this debilitating weapon the British were hopeful of inflicting similar discomfort on the German defenders whose gas masks were thought to offer inferior protection against the poisonous irritant.[10] One battery of the 55th Field Artillery Regiment attached to the German 75th Reserve Division was forced out of its positions due to heavy casualties from the gas attack. Twenty-one of its personnel were rendered unfit for action.[11] When the artillery returns were compiled after the battle they showed that a staggering 1,299,467 rounds had been fired into the German lines.[12]

Another dimension to the artillery support was the establishment of flying columns. As Monash explained in regard to the Australian divisions:

> Every one of the six brigades is accompanied by a brigade of artillery. Instead of these having to come out of the barrage they are tonight already camped with their infantry – horses guns and all . . . In addition to these six brigades each division has a mobile group of horse artillery – horse-drawn 6-pdrs and horse-drawn 6-inch Vickers naval guns. These will be used for counterbattery work.[13]

The success in recent operations had led both Monash and Rawlinson to believe that the Germans would not withstand the initial bombardment. At the 19 September meeting Monash had declared that the operation was 'more a matter of engineering and organisation than of fighting'. To Major-General John Gellibrand, commanding Monash's old 3rd Division, this comment suggested a belief in corps headquarters that the German position was little more than a machine-gun bluff.[14] It is certain that the senior British and Australian

9

commanders did not consider the German divisions holding this portion of the line to be of particularly high calibre. Of eight German divisions in the line on 29 September only one was considered as first class while of the six supporting divisions two were held to be so.[15] Rawlinson claimed he would never have contemplated attacking the Hindenburg Line had it not been for the marked deterioration of German morale over the past month. He thought the line would have been impregnable if defended by the Germans of two years ago.[16]

To hasten the battle along, Monash also planned for engineers and field companies to follow closely behind the infantry to construct and repair roads to allow artillery and supplies quick passage forward to keep pressure on the Germans. Four approach roads, two per divisional sector, were pencilled in on the maps with various units allocated specific sections to maintain. In the 27th Division, or northern sector, the roads were delineated as the Blue and Yellow roads. The northernmost was the Blue road and led from Lempire to Gillemont Farm. Below it was the Yellow road, which ran southeast from Ronssoy down to Malakoff Farm before jagging northeastward to Bony and on to Grand Court. In the 30th Division's sector they were Red and Black. The Red road ran from Hargicourt then north of Bellicourt through Cabaret Farm. Further south the Black road passed Bellicourt and led up to Nauroy. The roads were colour coded on the maps and painted posts were placed along the roadsides to assist with identification.[17]

The plan required much mutual assistance from the various arms. In the northern sector the Australian 3rd Pioneer Battalion would work with a company from the American 102nd Engineers.[18] Trucks would deliver road stone to be shovelled into damaged sections. Tanks would move alongside the roads compressing the ground to allow the passage of mule-drawn traffic.[19] In the southern section the Australian 5th Pioneer Battalion would work similarly with the American 105th Engineers and Australian 2nd Tunnelling Company. On the eve of the battle Monash declared that he did not think these roads would be adequate to supply the corps.[20] However before the plans for the attack on the Bellicourt Tunnel could be enacted it was first necessary to reconfigure the Fourth Army line.

During the night of the 20/21 September the 46th Territorial Division of the British IX Corps began to move into position south of the tunnel defences at Bellicourt. They thus became the right flank of the Fourth Army replacing the Australian 4th Division, which moved back towards Tincourt preparatory to a further movement to the rest area around Amiens. As the veteran Australians passed rearward their green American replacements were being bused and trained to their concentration points around Tincourt and Haut-Allaines prior to marching to the front line. Meanwhile the Australian 1st Division had sidestepped to its left to hold the line opposite the southern portion of the tunnel sector. On the night of 23/24 September the lead regiments of the American 30th Division began to relieve the Australian 1st Division, which followed the 4th Division into the rest areas. For the first time in nearly six months no Australian division held a position in the front line.

The following evening the American 27th Division relieved the centre and right of the British III Corps opposite the as yet unconquered spurs of the Hindenburg outpost line. The realignment of the Fourth Army front was virtually complete. On the morning of 25 September command control of the tunnel sector front passed to John Monash's Australian–American Corps.[21] The Australian 3rd and 5th Divisions did not move into their bivouac positions behind the American divisions until the evening of 27/28 September. On the same night the Australian 2nd Division was bused from Cappy to the Peronne area to act as the Corps reserve.[22]

The main area of concern for the proposed preliminary operation by the Americans lay directly in the 27th Division's 4,000-yard front, which was overlooked by the Knoll on the left, Gillemont Farm in the centre and Quennemont Farm on the right. The Germans also occupied the Malakoff Woods south of Quennemont Farm from which they were able to enfilade the 27th Division's right flank and the 30th Division's left. Apart from that

11

disagreeable situation the 30th Division was able to advance to within 500 yards of the outpost line on the morning of 26 September. As a result of this gain it would be spared the initial hardships to which its New York compatriots would soon be exposed.

This part of the Hindenburg outpost line was, unbeknownst to the defenders holding it, playing with marked psychological effect on the attackers. The reason, in part, extended back some months to when the British III Corps had suffered a torrid time in the August counteroffensive. It had been forced to undertake the sort of preliminary operation the Americans were now being called on to conduct when it had hurriedly to recast its battle plan thirty-six hours before the main assault to regain ground captured by the Australians a couple of weeks earlier, ground that had subsequently been reoccupied by the Germans. Although successful in August they had been left exhausted for the main assault and failed to keep to the timetable for the securing of their objectives. This failure had not gone unnoticed among the Australians. At Chipilly Spur a six-man Australian patrol played a pivotal role in leading English troops on to their objectives, the success of which only further fuelled an already highly charged disdain towards English troops held by the Australians.[23]

Now, in a new push, the III Corps were again found wanting. It made several attempts to capture its allocated section of the Hindenburg outpost line. By 19 September the ground had still not been made. With this failure Butler once again turned to the neighbouring Australians for assistance. As fate would have it the 1 Brigade of the Australian 1st Division was being relieved in the adjacent sector and the 1st Battalion – from which the famous six-man patrol had come – was asked to return to the line to make another attack. During the evening of 20 September a large portion of the 1st Battalion, 119 of just over 200 then in the line, refused to draw ammunition to carry out an attack at Ruby Wood. Officers could not persuade the men to fight and the disaffected soldiers opted to walk out of the line stating they would have been

12

prepared to hold their trenches (had their officers been agreeable) but would not attack as they had done enough and that they were being asked to do the work of others. This was not the first sign of a potentially parlous situation developing in the Australian ranks. Six days beforehand three platoons of the 59th Battalion, supported by their officers, refused to re-enter the line after having just been relieved.[24]

Compounding these unfortunate outbreaks of mutiny was an army directive received on 19 September immediately to reduce the number of battalions from four to three in the Australian brigades. After consultation with his divisional commanders Monash designated seven battalions for disbandment. Those nominated were the 19th, 21st, 25th, 37th, 42nd, 54th and 60th Battalions. The order was fiercely resisted by the affected formations. Spokesmen for these battalions argued that they had started the war and won honours under their unit's banner and that it was only fair that they finish the job under the same. The general mood among the troops was recorded by one digger in his diary:

> Everyone's sentiments is with the boys – to think of any Bn [batallion] dying out after the years, now, of fighting done by it, is hard on those men who have made the excellent name everyone of our Bns bear – and it should be for the boys themselves to judge – had they spoken of breaking this Bn up, we too should have cried it down . . . Feeling everywhere is far from peaceful . . . those that have been through the lot badly need and deserve a rest. Expect, however, that more decorations are still required by the heads.[25]

Given the grievances being aired by the 1st and 59th Battalions the possibility exists that some men in the other battalions seized on the admirable sentiment of *esprit de corps* as a means to try and gain what they considered was a well-earned rest. Irrespective of the motivations of the various mutineers, these were

13

distractions Monash did not need as he prepared to integrate the Americans to his command and plan for the forthcoming battle.

The possibility of industrial action *en masse* – for that was how the soldiers saw it – was not a fanciful notion given the comments of another Australian soldier:

> Things were getting v. serious as the trouble was spreading to the artillery and other arms and a general strike was well in sight and all were heartily sick of being continuously promised a spell which never came.[26]

After nearly a week of protracted resistance from the men, Monash prevailed on Haig and Rawlinson to allow another fortnight's grace so that the pending operation might not be threatened by a sympathy strike by other battalions.[27]

Once the Fourth Army realignment had been completed, planning for the battle began in earnest. On 23 September Monash delivered a three-hour exposition to the Americans of the plan of battle and requirements of the line commanders. Major-General John F. O'Ryan remembered it being so 'detailed that there did not seem to be necessity to ask many questions.'[28] Three days later Monash gathered the staff and line officers of the Australian–American Corps in conference to go over the entire plan. Haig arrived towards the end of this two-and-a-half-hour meeting and, at Monash's insistence, spoke to the American commanders delivering words of encouragement for the forthcoming fight.

There seems no doubt that Monash was feeling greater anxiety about this operation above any other over which he had presided. His uncertainty about the ability of the Americans, his doubts for the success of the IX Corps frontal assault and the fraying morale issues in his own command were all gnawing at his mind. The pressure would manifest itself in some intemperate outbursts towards subordinates during the battle.

14

To assist the integration of American method to the mores of Australian planning, a detachment of seasoned Australian officers and NCOs was attached to the American divisions. This was variously called the American mission or Australian mission, though the latter was most used, and was headed by Brigadier-General Sinclair-MacLagan. It consisted of 87 officers and 127 NCOs drawn from the Australian 1st and 4th Divisions. Brigadier-General Brand would lead a detachment of 4th Division men and assist the 27th Division. Brigadier-General Iven Mackay would assist the 30th Division with his 1st Division detachment.

Sinclair-MacLagan, who was regarded as somewhat superficial and boastful by one American observer, was attached to Read's II Corps headquarters with Brand and Mackay advising the respective American divisional headquarters to which they were attached.[29] Officers were distributed among the American brigade headquarters with four NCOs attached to each battalion, one per company, to advise on logistics and tactical matters.

The mission joined the Americans on 24 September. The Australian role was to be of an advisory nature only and carried with it no executive power. It was for the Americans to decide what would work best for their troops though it was obvious that the opinions of Australian veterans were regarded highly. The prime purpose of the mission was to assist in the preparation for the attack of 29 September. Australian officers and NCOs supervised the taping of start lines and positioning of troops. The commander of the American 54 Infantry Brigade, Brigadier-General Palmer E. Pierce, was particularly thankful for the invaluable services and lessons the Australians provided in regard to matters of supply, including the provision of hot meals to the men at the front.[30] The NCOs were recalled on 28 September but the officers remained until after the main attack had begun.

One task undertaken by the Australian intelligence officers was to supervise the production of contour maps to familiarise the officers and men with the ground over which the regiments had to attack. In the case of the American

15

107th Regiment, these maps were never completed as the unit was ordered forward and few of its personnel saw even the incomplete version.[31]

According to Private Willard M. Newton of the American 105th Engineer Train he was able to glean from the Australians 'lots of things that are important to a soldier who has not been in battle'. It was clear, too, that the impressionable doughboys were uncritically accepting of Australian claims of German 'torture' and 'extreme cruelty' towards their prisoners.[32] On such issues the Australians' veteran status gave added credibility as Newton noted, 'We believe them, for they have been in this war long enough to know.'[33] The Australian advice was not to allow oneself to be captured or, as Newton implied, to take no prisoners: 'They have no use for the Huns.'[34]

How valuable the mission's contribution was in the final outcome of the American phase of operations is difficult to appraise. Sinclair-MacLagan claimed in his congratulatory orders that it was undoubtedly responsible for the success achieved by the American II Corps.[35] American commanders also acknowledged the valuable assistance proffered. Given the massive problems that engulfed the Americans when battle was joined and the long list of improvements to American planning and organisation suggested by Brand and McKay after the battle, in truth the mission was only able to achieve minimal influence.

The preliminary operation of the Americans to capture the remaining section of the Hindenburg outpost line, in which some of the Australian mission became embroiled, was set for the morning of 27 September. It was thought this would allow sufficient time for them to secure the jumping-off point for the main attack. It seems too great a premium was placed on the supposed poor morale of the Germans and not enough given to the fact that the advance of two British divisions, the 18th and 74th – irrespective of what claims might be made on their quality – had been arrested with heavy casualties by the German resistance in this sector. Final instructions for the preliminary operation and main battle were delivered at the conference on the morning of 26 September. With the meeting's conclusion no alterations would be allowed.

CHAPTER TWO

The Preliminary Operation

'Get this done quickly!' – Major Gillett, American 106th Regiment

The weather forecast for 27 September was uninviting. Overcast skies and a slight fog were predicted. At 5.30 a.m. soldiers of the American 106th Regiment, 27th Division, were scheduled to advance towards the three spurs overlooking their position. The regiment was formerly the 23rd New York Regiment, with service in the American Civil War and Mexican Border War, and it was now about to add another chapter to its colourful history.

This vital attack did not lack considered planning. Nine brigades of artillery would provide a creeping barrage that included a fifteen per cent mix of smoke shells. A special allotment of one company of twelve tanks from the 4th Tank Battalion would advance with the three infantry battalions. The 27th Division front extended 4,000 yards and required a 1,000-yard advance. On the left flank British patrols from the 12th Division, III Corps would assist with minor advances. They were not to make a general attack but merely to conform to the advance of the Americans, getting forwards wherever circumstances permitted.[1] The left flank moving against the Knoll would receive added support from two companies of the American 105th Regiment, which were to hold a defensive flank behind them. As well, detachments from the 102nd Engineers and 102nd Field Service units would accompany the advance. Extra support would be provided from the 104th and 106th Machine Gun Battalions. The Australian 4th Divisional Artillery was directly to assist the 27th Division

19

in the three sub-sectors as needed after the protective barrage lifted.[2] On the right the American 30th Division would continue to push forward following its success of the previous day. By mid-morning the American 118th Regiment had advanced the line with relative ease to the Brown Line except on its left near Malakoff Farm where it was enfiladed by enemy machine guns operating from the 27th Division's sector. This was an ominous portent of the day that lay ahead.

A general bombardment of the German line had commenced the previous evening in preparation for the main attack in two days' time. For twelve hours the enemy was deluged with mustard gas. The British guns then switched their attention to shelling all known artillery positions as well as the approach roads in the back areas with a view to disrupting the supply of materials and reinforcements to the threatened front. German prisoners taken subsequently attested to the effectiveness of the barrage. Many units suffered heavy casualties although it appears those sustained from the gas attack varied, being considered only slight in many areas.[3]

The greater portion of the bombardment was reserved for flattening and destroying the massed barbed-wire entanglements that the Germans had erected in front of their lines. These were five bands deep in some places. A new shell had become available to assist in this task. An instantaneous fuse known as the '106 Fuse' was able to be affixed to shells and explode on contact with the slightest obstacle such as a strand of wire. The beauty of this innovation was that the shell exploded above the ground avoiding the creation of craters which further inhibited the advance of supporting troops. As well, the multi-directional percussion of the blast uprooted wire entanglements and blew them aside in a jumbled mass.[4]

The men of the American 106th Regiment filed across fields and byways to reach the assembly line an hour before zero. Taped start lines had been laid and secured the previous night by patrols sent out for that purpose. They dumped their overcoats, blankets and kits at their company headquarters and moved into the forward area. Unfortunately some of the companies found their movement illuminated by Very lights. Startled by this occurrence and the manner in which night turned to day they continued to move. Experienced soldiers would have stopped hoping to pass as inanimate objects. Pale green SOS rockets shot into the sky and an intensive machine-gun barrage descended on the Americans. Already struggling in the pitch black to find the assembly points this unexpected outbreak of violence added another layer of discomfort to their journey. Some units were not organised along the start line until five minutes before zero hour but all were ready when the supporting barrage fell.[5]

Those lying on the tapes were encouraged by the noise and flashing guns of the general bombardment. They had endured a harrowing night with the Germans launching some raids in strength to test and identify the troops now facing them.[6] Each man carried five grenades on his person as well as a raincoat and rations. The American 106th Regiment was part of the 53 Brigade. Numerically it was the weaker of its three sister regiments. Nevertheless with forty-one officers and 2,037 other ranks it was the equivalent of two full Australian battalions and, given the attrition rates to that late stage in the war, few of the Australian brigades of four battalions could put that many effectives into the line.

The regiment was to attack on a three-battalion front each of 1,000–1,500 yards width. The distance to the German lines varied but for the most part lay approximately a thousand yards due east of the start line. Through a desire to preserve as much of the 27th Division for the main assault, Monash had initially stipulated that the regiment was to be the sole infantry involved. However a decision was arrived at soon after planning commenced to attach elements of the American 105th Regiment in support.[7]

The 106th Regiment lined up from right to left with its first battalion opposite Quennemont Farm, the second in the centre facing Gillemont Farm and the third on the left in front of the Knoll. Two companies formed each battalion's front with a third in reserve. Each battalion's front line was supplemented with three Mark V tanks and a fourth tank in reserve carrying supplies to be dumped in the forward area. Also, a platoon of four machine guns from the regiment's machine-gun company would move forward with each battalion. Liaison between all units was to be from right to left.

Opposing the Americans in this sector was the German IV Reserve Corps. Its headquarters were in Guoy. The 8th Division held Vendhuille with the 72nd Regiment holding the northern part of its front and the 153rd Regiment protecting the town opposite the British front. The 54th Division, commanded by General Kabisch, faced off against the northern half of the American sector with the 84th Schleswig-Holstein Infantry Regiment on the Knoll, the 27th Reserve Infantry Regiment above Gillemont Farm and the 90th Reserve Infantry Regiment below. Further south was the 121st Division with its three regiments – the 7th, 56th and 60th – holding the outpost trenches running north to south to a point just above Bellicourt.[8]

At zero hour the supporting barrage from 18-pounders firing three rounds per minute fell like a fiery curtain 100 yards forward of the start line. Two hundred yards beyond it 4.5 inch-howitzers firing two rounds per minute laid another screen. After three minutes the protective barrage commenced the first of 100-yard lifts creeping towards the German outpost position. Twenty minutes later the density of the barrage would decrease to a single round per minute.[9]

Thirty-six minutes had been allowed for the Americans to make the outpost line and a further thirty-nine minutes for consolidation through which period the barrage would lie 400 yards east of the captured position in a protective screen. Critically, though, many Germans in the outpost line had survived the general barrage and held their nerve. They knew the strength of the position having resisted all attempts by the British III Corps in previous days. Furthermore, the Germans were quickly able to organise a retaliatory barrage on the advancing line of Americans. Given the potentially crippling counterbattery fire they knew would be directed against them, the German artillerymen were quickly supplied to maximise their rate of fire in case of destruction. In addition, many German machine-gun posts had been sited forward of the high ground and occupied the area over which the Americans must advance. Thus the Americans were immediately engaged and suffering casualties.

It is interesting to consider the assessments being made of German morale at this time. Generally it was felt that the infantry were demoralised having suffered heavily over the past months. The artillerymen though were thought to have been in better spirits having been the beneficiaries of better food and billets in the back areas. The heavy machine-gun companies were usually formidable, maintaining their full complement of sixteen guns. Infantry companies by contrast were depleted. Some numbered as few as twenty-five men while others could count as many as sixty, at most, in the line. The majority of companies fell between those marks and possessed three to five light machine guns.[10]

The American 106th Regiment went forward with the importance of the operation impressed on them. The divisional commander had issued detailed orders of his expectations. Among them was the need to hold the line irrespective of casualties or weather conditions.[11] Rain had fallen the previous night making the ground slippery but it was a long way from the quagmires of a year ago. The weather was of grave concern to the senior military planners whose memories were scorched by the disastrous effects the early rains had on operations the previous year. Nearly twelve months had passed but already the name of Passchendaele was synonymous with mud and untold suffering.

The initial progress of the Americans was good. Despite a heavy artillery counterbarrage and equally severe machine-gun fire, they clung to the fringe of the protective barrage and reached the vicinity of their main objectives. Mist in some parts of the area also assisted in screening the attackers' exact whereabouts. On the extreme left and rear the two supporting companies of

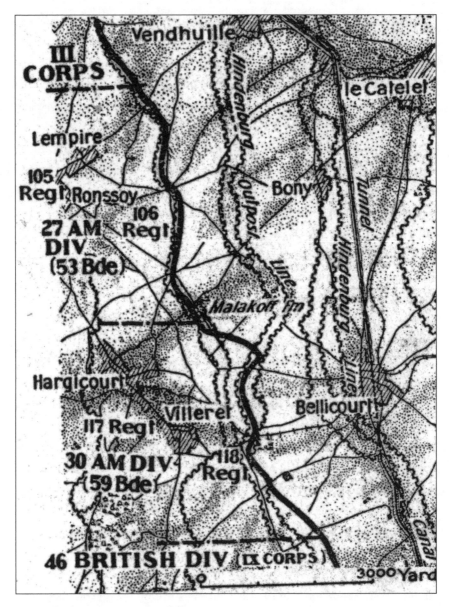

MAP 3 *The American position prior to the preliminary attack*

the 105th Regiment, companies K and M, reached Crellin Trench and formed a defensive line there. They signalled their success at 6.05 a.m., thirty-five minutes after zero hour. Ahead of them the 3rd Battalion, 106th Regiment was warmly engaged as it attempted to push towards the Knoll.

At 53 Brigade headquarters and subsequently at 27th Division headquarters a picture of success was emerging about the fighting on the left. By 7.15 a.m. brigade was confirming success on the Knoll with the capture of between 125 and 150 prisoners. The German prisoners belonged to the 3rd Battalion, 84th Regiment and two forward companies of the 27th Regiment. They had been cut off in the light mist as the Americans and supporting tanks passed between the Knoll and Gillemont Farm.[12] The capture of prisoners was further corroborated by observers from the Australian artillery. Supplies from the supporting tank were dropped at the front line and the tank officers, after driving about the Knoll, returned and reported all well there.[13]

One soldier thankful for the American success was a British subaltern belonging to the 10th Essex. Wounded in a previous attack, he had lain for three days in a shell hole nursing his shattered leg while the fury of the Allied bombardments swept over him. He was eventually carried to safety.[14]

The American success was however short-lived. It seems the majority of the 3rd Battalion, 106th Regiment had been halted by heavy fire about a hundred yards short of the main German line and its attack became one of disconnected and isolated squads pushing forward. One band of about forty men under Lieutenant Turner from M Company, 105th Regiment, bombed, bayoneted and shot their way through the German lines and passed over and beyond the Knoll position. However separated as they were from the main attacking body, they were completely without support. One company of counterattacking Germans from the 27th Regiment claimed they passed by one group of Americans in trenches in that area. These may have been Turner's band.

Corporal White of M Company was sent rearwards to find aid and gain further instructions. As he made his way back he came on Germans in strength in a trench and dugouts. These had either been bypassed initially in the American advance due to the fog or been sent forwards as reinforcements. At any rate White had to act quickly. Relying on bluff alone he jumped boldly on the parapet and called loudly for their surrender. The surprised Germans complied, expecting greater numbers of doughboys to appear behind the animated American. Some one hundred filed out of the trenches to the relative safety of captivity. Though successful in this spectacular solo performance, White's mission was not accomplished and Turner and his diminishing band were left to go it alone.[15]

At the Knoll the leading groups of Americans were driven out of their positions by determined German counterattacks. Reserve companies of the 27th and 84th Regiments were brought forward from the main Hindenburg Line. They were joined in a counterattack by isolated portions of the 27th Regiment, which had been bypassed in the initial assault. The Americans resisted with machine-gun fire initially but soon succumbed to a combined bombing and rifle grenade attack. According to the Germans the Americans displayed a marked lack of experience appearing 'unskilled in attack' and 'helpless' in close fighting.[16] The testimony of American soldiers painted a rather contradictory picture about their skill with the bayonet and the superiority of the Mill's grenade over the German 'potato masher' in close quarter fighting.[17]

One problem associated with the Knoll, which was nothing more than a flat expanse of open ground scoured with trenches set on a rise, was that it was dominated by the heights northeast of Vendhuille.[18] It lay within easy reach of German reinforcements coming up from their main line. These soon crowded in on the advanced elements of the 106th Regiment, also striking the right side of the two companies of the 105th Regiment (K and M) drawn up in support. The remnants of the 3rd Battalion, 106th Regiment attack companies were forced off their gains and fell back on Company K, 105th Regiment adjacent to the British 12th Division sector. The tanks that reported the Knoll in American possession must have done so after finding Turner's men on the objective.

The line was eventually withdrawn to within 300 yards of the jumping-off line. Given the obscure nature of things the commanding officer of the 3rd Battalion, 106th Regiment, Captain Blaisdell, hurried to the front line from battalion headquarters late in the morning to try to retrieve the situation. In the meantime the reserve companies of the 105th Regiment were being pushed forward. A counterattack of survivors of the 106th Regiment and men from Companies L and I of the 105th, with artillery and machine-gun support, succeeded in pushing the advancing Germans back to the line of Tombois Trench north of the Knoll.[19]

In the centre and on the right it appears that 1st Battalion, 106th Regiment and 2nd Battalion, 106th Regiment carried portions of the outpost line trenches but were unable to overcome the defenders holding the farm strongholds. Gillemont Farm was defended by the 90th Regiment. By 7.05 a.m. they had beaten down all attacks north of the farm. An hour later they counterattacked south of the farm and captured about fifty doughboys.[20]

Unable to break down the farm defences, the 2nd Battalion, 106th Regiment was left occupying Claymore Trench which ran north to south and slightly southeast of the farm. They were receiving fire from the farm and from Gillemont Trench, which ran southwards from it. It is difficult to know exactly what occurred here. Had the Americans passed over Gillemont Trench into Claymore Trench or had they held it and been driven out by Germans being fed into the Gillemont Trench from the farm position? They might, too, have struck Claymore Trench while moving well south of the farm and bombed their way up. By midday it was clear that the 2nd Battalion, 106th Regiment was in a precarious position as the Germans in considerable strength at the farm had succeeded in interposing a line in rear of the Americans. The supporting tanks managed to circle the farm but found it too strongly defended to make inroads. They did however report successfully quelling some machine-gun posts and capturing some prisoners who surrendered on their approach.[21] In

27

view of the resistance being displayed, 53 Brigade headquarters ordered the support companies up to try to quash the opposition there.[22]

On the right things had also been tough. The 1st Battalion, 106th Regiment carried the first line of trenches in front of Quennemont Farm but could get no further. The battalion commander, Major Ransom Hooker Gillett, called up Captain Henry Maslin's company of the 105th Regiment which was waiting in reserve. 'Get this done quickly,' urged Gillett as he sent Maslin's men off to attack the farm.[23] They were immediately counterattacked by the garrison troops of the 60th Regiment reinforced by half a company brought up from the Hindenburg Line. The Americans were forced back.[24] At 9.25 a.m., the 1st Battalion, 106th Regiment and supporting company held the trenches that ran southeast below Quennemont Farm to Malakoff Woods. They were trying to consolidate but could not because of heavy fire from the farm. No tanks had reached the forward positions with this battalion.

Of the twelve tanks that had been attached to the 106th Regiment, six were rendered unfit for service the next day. Artillery, machine-gun and anti-tank fire had been heavy. Three tanks were disabled from direct hits, two were ditched and the sixth made unserviceable after being badly damaged by anti-tank fire. The effectiveness of the tanks had been compromised by the weather. In the dark the crews had great difficulty in maintaining direction and in distinguishing friend from foe. Infantry guides had proved ineffectual. As daylight broke the machines also became more visible and were targeted with greater accuracy by the Germans. After the initial foray the tanks returned to their rallying point between the villages of Lempire and Ronssoy. They had expended 500 rounds of their six-pounder gun armament and 2,500 of small-arms ammunition. Later in the afternoon the tank battalion commander was summoned to 106th Regiment's headquarters to see if the tanks could assist the infantry forwards to their objectives. It was decided that the attempt to send them out over the ridge in full daylight would be too dangerous especially without sufficient artillery screening. A section of tanks was gathered and placed at the infantry's disposal for the next morning if required although this offer was eventually declined.[25]

As the morning wore into the afternoon the American position began to deteriorate in the Gillemont and Quennemont sectors as it had done around the Knoll. Losses among officers and NCOs had left many companies leaderless, which resulted in a loss of cohesion. Seventeen of the regiment's eighteen company officers were either killed or wounded on this day.[26] The position around Gillemont Farm in the centre remained critical all afternoon. The Americans hunkered down as best they could against the heavy fire being directed at them. Patrols from the support company of the 105th Regiment were pushed forward to make contact. However they brought no significant relief for the exhausted soldiers hanging on in the German trenches.

On the right 1st Battalion, 106th Regiment had lost contact with its headquarters and supporting troops. A heavy German attack was unleashed against them around 1 p.m. and thereafter no information was forthcoming as to what their position might be. Patrols from Company B, 105th Regiment, which had moved into the start line position earlier in the day, pushed forward at 7.30 p.m. in an attempt to make contact with the 106th Regiment. They made none.[27]

By the evening it was obvious to all that the objectives had not been taken and that the preliminary operation must necessarily be extended into the next day if the jumping-off positions for the main attack were to be secured. The exact whereabouts of the American line was subject to some conjecture. Contact with the front line troops was minimal. Amazingly a verbal report was delivered at 6.30 p.m. by an officer returning from the front line to the effect that the Knoll, Gillemont Farm and Quennemont Farm were in American possession with only pockets of the enemy remaining to be mopped up.[28]

Aerial reconnaissance told a vastly different story. Between 11.15 a.m. and 12.15 p.m. an aeroplane contact patrol had flown over the objective line in a bid to have ground troops respond with signal flares. None was seen. Another pass was made at 5.30 p.m. and again no contact was made. In fact only one signal disc was spotted. These were metal discs cut from biscuit tins and attached to the underside of the flap on the soldiers' small box respirators. When the reconnaissance planes sounded a Morse A on their Klaxon horns the ground troops were meant to display the discs and set off their signal flares if they had them. What the planes were able to determine in a later sweep was that the Americans were forward of the morning's jump-off position in a rough diagonal line running from south and west of the Quennemont Farm on the right, with some groups in the centre around the southwestern outskirts of Gillemont Farm from where the line jagged back sharply to the left almost to the start line west of the Knoll.[29]

Casualties had been heavy. Based on the next morning's returns 1st Battalion, 106th Regiment had been reduced from 497 officers and men to 198, 2nd Battalion, 106th Regiment from 525 to 246 and 3rd Battalion, 106th Regiment from 496 to 214.[30] This represented losses of 60 per cent, 47 per cent and 67 per cent respectively and was consistent with those sustained in any major battle. At day's end it had to be said that the Germans had held their own admirably in this sector.

The troops participating in the main assault were due to move into the line that evening and next morning. Clearly this was compromised in the 27th Division sector. The 54 Brigade had set off on its approach march from the Tincourt area as fighting raged along the 27th Division front on 27 September. They were to relieve the 53 Brigade in accordance with the main plan of battle. The relief began in the early hours of 28 September with strong patrols pushing forwards with the dual intention of making contact with the remnants of the 106th Regiment and advancing the start line as far forwards as possible. In neither were they particularly successful. With the exception of one officer and seven men of the 106th found in the Quennemont Farm area, nothing more was known about those reported on the objective the previous day.[31]

The 54 Brigade relieved the 53 Brigade and occupied the 27th Division sector on a two-regiment front. The 107th Regiment was assigned the left, north of Gillemont Farm to the Knoll and the III Corps boundary. The 108th Regiment was allocated the right, south of Gillemont Farm to Quennemont Farm and beyond to the American 30th Division's left boundary. Here on the extreme right several enemy outposts were located and with artillery support were driven out and the line advanced to within 200 yards of the 27th Division's actual jump-off line. Two battalions of each regiment formed the front line with the third in reserve. The 53 Brigade became the divisional reserve with the 105th Regiment supporting the 108th on the right and the remnants of the 106th forming a composite battalion to support the 107th on the left.

The British had tried to support the American left by pushing forwards towards the canal and Vendhuille northeast of the Knoll. They too had met with heavy fire. Progress was slow. The Germans were strongly entrenched in Lark Trench and the quarries nearby.[32] A more determined attack was planned for the next day by the British 12th Division as suppressing the German defenders in Vendhuille was recognised as being critical to the support of operations against the Knoll and other trenches in that portion of the outpost line.

On 28 September, zero hour was set for 5 a.m. and the British 37 Brigade was to make the attack, the object being a line just west of the canal. The 6th Buffs and 6th Royal West Kents led off on the right and left respectively. The Buffs were followed by the 9th Battalion of the Essex Regiment and the Royal West Kents by the 6th Queens. After a short sharp bombardment the men advanced. They were met by the same stiff resistance offered the previous day. Fighting lasted all day and eventually a gradual gain was made. The Buffs succeeded in pushing the Germans out of the quarries and by late afternoon they alone had reached the designated objective west of the canal. They captured 120 prisoners and forty machine guns but had been unable to stop the German fire emanating from Vendhuille.[33]

While the infantry battled to make up the ground, the general artillery programme continued all along the line. The barrage was described in one German divisional history as a 'fearful, systematic bombardment'.[34] Throughout the day combat patrols from the American 54 Brigade worked diligently in patchy drizzling rain under an intermittent artillery and machine-gun fire. They failed to gain contact with any survivors from the 106th Regiment who were thought to be occupying isolated posts as far forward as Willow Trench.[35]

The American 107th Regiment was camped in Kent Lane from where it looked out on the morally disarming sight of the dead from previous attacks. So grotesque were some of these that Captain Claude G. Leland of Company I arranged to have some of his men take gunny sacks out to cover the staring sightless eyes of the dead. The men were ordered to rest as best they could in the cold conditions while fatigue parties worked to improve the shelter in the lane with timber and sheets of iron.[36]

In the evening the 54 Brigade commander advised that his men had pegged out a jump-off line and expected to reach a distance of 400 yards behind the barrage line for the main attack. A reconnoitring patrol from Company K suffered heavy loss when it attempted to crawl out to the Knoll position to feel out the enemy position. Fired on from many directions it struggled back to the main line.[37] On the advice of the Australian officers with the American units it was decided that the advanced positioning of the jump-off tapes was too unsafe and that they needed to be pulled back virtually to the old start position – 1,000 yards short of the enemy line.[38]

By far the most crucial event of this day was played out in the headquarters of the 54 Brigade. There, at noon, General John O'Ryan – the 27th Division commander – and his chief of staff met with General Monash's representative, Brigadier-General Brand of the Australian mission. Aerial reconnaissance reports from the 3rd and 35th Air Squadrons made at 11 a.m. and 11.30 a.m. respectively had brought mixed information. Both Gillemont Farm and Quennemont Farm were reported as appearing to be deserted. It is likely that this *was* in appearance only. Some Germans were sighted north and south of Gillemont Farm with about two hundred occupying the sunken road that bore off northwest from the farm across the Dirk valley to Bony. Further south heavy fire was reported issuing from a line that roughly accorded with a position that ran from Quennet Copse, through Quennemont Farm to the Malakoff Woods. Along this line the Germans were obviously holding on in some strength. The 108th Regiment's report of unusual activity in their front corroborates this and the heavy barrage brought down by the enemy in the afternoon was proof that an alert foe lay before them.

The more intriguing aspect of the air contact reports was the sightings that placed American troops around the Knoll and east of Gillemont Farm.[39] It seems likely that this was a case of mistaken identity or that those seen were clusters of American dead or wounded. Aerial reconnaissance can be considered only an inexact science given that men from the 46th Division were strafed by their own planes during the main attack the next day.[40] If there were any Americans in the reported positions they were certainly not having any appreciable effect on the German resistance which was preventing the 107th Regiment getting forward to the jump-off line.

With half the day elapsed it was obvious to all at the conference that the start line for the 29 September attack was not going to be reached. A proposition was put forward that the artillery barrage be pulled back to allow the 27th Division troops to advance under its protection. The previous day the 106th Regiment had at least got close enough to its objectives in the initial phase to suggest that with double the troops in the line the 54 Brigade must have had a good chance of success if this was done. However after consultation with the artillery commander it was decided that such a change to the barrage plan was impracticable in the short time available – though it surely could have been arranged in the available twelve or more hours by a dedicated G staff. The reconnaissance reports that placed American troops around the Knoll and Gillemont Farm ended any further talk on the matter. The idea of bringing down a barrage on his own men was simply repugnant to O'Ryan and to the mass of his command. The American commanders would not countenance application of such cynical tactical logic.

In view of the uncertainty in front of the 27th Division, representation was then made to General Monash as to the possibility of delaying the operation a day to allow the ground to be made up. Monash was supportive of this idea and hastened to the army commander. Rawlinson however decided that there could be no substantial alteration to the plan. Extra tanks would be provided for the 27th Division to compensate for the lack of artillery cover. Rawlinson claimed that this was preferable suggesting that the Americans, having had no real experience of sticking to a creeping barrage, would stick to the advancing tanks that would be attached to the leading battalions. This was errant nonsense as the 106th Regiment had clearly demonstrated the previous day that the doughboys, green as they were, were quite capable of staying with a creeping barrage line.[41]

Rawlinson's refusal to allow the Australian–American Corps operation to be postponed had left the Australian commander in a state of visible anxiety. Monash had for some time been feeling the fraying effects of continued service. He had asked his army commander for some leave at the start of September but his request was declined. There is nothing to suggest that Monash was approaching a debilitating state but he was certainly exhibiting signs of irritability and impatience which he might otherwise have kept in check. Haig visited the Australian headquarters at 3 p.m. where he found Monash in what he described as a self-confessed state of despair. Monash obviously made it known to his disapproving commander-in-chief that he felt the American attack would fail and that he held little confidence in the IX Corps' chances of forcing the canal on the American 30th Division's right. Haig tried to calm Monash's disquiet with reassuring words to the effect that the situation was not as serious as the Australian commander imagined it to be and that the attack should go ahead as planned. Later that evening Monash addressed a group of war correspondents on the details of the operation in which he laid particular stress on the likelihood of failure by the Americans to gain their objectives.[42]

On 29 September the attacking units in the 27th Division sector were to form an hour before zero and try to fight their way to the designated start line by zero hour. The supporting bombardment would fall on its originally planned line behind the Knoll, Gillemont Farm and Quennemont Farm strongholds.[43] That meant the German defenders holding those positions would be largely free of artillery interference with a clear field of fire over the 1,000 yards leading to their positions. This did not bode well for the success of the division.

When the first news of the impossibility of bringing the barrage back was received by the 107th Regiment it came like a dose of bitter medicine. Captain Leland discussed the situation with a friend and concluded that the regiment was to be sacrificed with very little prospect of survival for the men. These glum tidings were soothed mildly by information brought later in the evening stating that tanks would go forward with them to crush the wire and silence machine guns.[44] Only the morrow would reveal whether the optimistic or pessimistic outlook would hold sway. If there existed any consolation it might have been that the British 46th Division on the right flank had been set a seemingly equally daunting task.

CHAPTER THREE

46th North Midland Division

'Winning the war' – British commanding officer

The job of forcing the canal on the right flank of Monash's corps had fallen to the 46th North Midland Division. The Division's regiments represented the very heart of 'old England'. Monash had a contingency plan in place should they fail. The 59 Brigade of the American 30th Division was to form a defensive line behind the American's right flank.[1] Of course, if the canal defences were unable to be forced then the advancing 30th Division's right flank would be open to enfilade from the German positions depending on how well the 59 Brigade could perform as a refused defensive flank.

The 46th Division was commanded by Major-General Gerald Boyd. He believed his division's role was at best a sacrificial stunt with no greater expectation than gaining a foothold on the other side of the canal.[2] On the face of it the task set had little to commend it. The division had to cross a substantial body of water, through the fire zones of numerous enemy machine-gun posts dug into the steep embankments up which the attackers had to climb once across the canal. This section of the line was like a huge trough and it was easy to imagine what a slaughter pen it could become if troops were pushed into it and the machine guns above were not silenced.

Two factors would work in favour of the British attack. The first was planned for and constituted the artillery pounding all likely defensive positions south of the tunnel, most of which had been gleaned from the captured documents of the Hindenburg Line. The second was unforeseen and came in the guise of a dense fog which blanketed the battlefield reducing visibility to only a few yards for a period of nearly two hours.

If the commanders of this division were gripped by a general pessimism surrounding their chances of success then they did not show it. Boyd was an enthusiastic innovator. He had entered the army as a private in 1895 and he never lost sight of the needs of the common infantryman. Great effort was made to ensure a successful assault. The men were provided with a variety of devices to assist their passage across the canal. Mud mats, collapsible boats, rafts, steel lines with blocks and cordage as well as life jackets and nine-foot scaling ladders. All were carried by the leading brigade. The boats, rafts and mats each required sixteen to twenty men to carry them. The assaulting 137 Brigade must have presented a strange sight as it lumbered across the fields with its cargo to the start line. The vast majority within the division could not swim. To allay their fear of drowning, demonstrations of how a fully armed soldier in a life jacket could cross safely were conducted prior to the operation in the Somme river.[3]

The 46th Division was to start from the Hindenburg outpost line and reach its first objective, which constituted the captured German canal defence from the main Estrees Road (Watling Street on most maps) to the outskirts of Bellenglise. Once the 137 Brigade was consolidated on that line it would advance to its next objective, which was the trench system that ran northwest of Magny la Fosse across Springbok valley over Knobkerry Ridge and then bent back towards Bullet Copse. Hereabouts it would link with a detachment of the 1st Division moving in support from Bellenglise to provide a defensive flank. The 138 and 139 Brigades would then extend the divisional line to a two-brigade front passing through the 137 Brigade on to the next objective. This was the Green Line, located east of Magny la Fosse and southwest of Joncourt and ran through Fosse Wood, over Lehaucourt Ridge into the Levergies valley.

Once this was gained the 32nd Division would continue the attack eastward to the Red Line.

The 46th Division made its way into the line on the evening and morning of 27/28 September. It formed up on a three-battalion front in the old German lines facing the canal south of the Riquevel entrant and just above Bellenglise. Prior to its arrival the 4th Leicestershire Regiment had pushed forward of the intended line to a distance of about 1,000 yards capturing a section of enemy trench on the high ground northwest of Bellenglise. Further north another section of ground was gained just east of Pike Woods. Companies from the incoming troops filed into these outpost positions during the night. The 6th North Staffordshire Regiment held the left and took over the advanced Pike Wood position while the 5th South Staffordshire Regiment was allocated the centre of the line and took over the newly captured trench section. As advantageous as high ground was to any military equation, outpost positions and salients were always vulnerable to concentrated enemy attack due to the flanks being exposed. The Germans here were not inclined benignly to concede this ground, which looked down on their canal defences.

At 7 a.m. on 28 September German bombers began working up the trench from the direction of Bellenglise showering the newly arrived troops with stick grenades. A fierce bombing encounter continued until 10 a.m. when the Germans attacked under cover of an artillery barrage. The 5th South Staffordshire fell back to a sunken road behind the trenches.

The 6th North Staffordshire was also attacked but hung on gamely using captured German bombs, guns and ammunition to supplement their own dwindling supplies. Messengers were sent back over the fire-swept ground behind them to seek replenishment but the severity of the German fire prevented supplies being carried forwards in the daylight. Fighting raged all day and by nightfall the 5th South Staffordshire had lost 150 men and the 6th North Staffordshire forty-five.[4] The two companies were withdrawn under cover of darkness. The 46th Division had had its nose bloodied but it was still on the designated start line ready to move forwards next morning.

The night of the 28/29 September was dark and windy. German guns were actively harassing the British front but their fire slackened as the night wore on. The darkness and wind gave way to a relatively fine and bright night. Half an hour prior to zero a thick mist rolled in enshrouding everything and blotting out all recognisable landmarks. Officers bringing their men forwards did so entirely with the aid of compasses. Remarkably, with few exceptions, the alignments were perfect.

The fog that enveloped the battlefield was a godsend to the attacking troops. It obviously caused some difficulty in gaining their bearings but this was a small price to pay for the total cover provided against direct observation from the enemy machine gunners and artillery observers. German observers simply could not determine if an attack was developing or not. The first inkling they had was when the supporting barrage swept like a cyclone across their positions. The weight of the barrage kept the defenders firmly ensconced in the concrete dugouts that honeycombed the canal's east bank. There were about fifty of these set above the high embankment that stretched from the tunnel's southern entrance to Bellenglise. The thickest cluster of dugouts was situated behind the quarry opposite the Riqueval Farm. Behind them on the forward slopes leading up to the village of Nauroy were situated a number of machine-gun posts. Further south another line of dugouts blocked the path into Springbok valley. The high ground behind it was laced with machine guns overlooking the main road to Estrees which, as with those protecting Nauroy, covered the line of any approach. It was a formidable defensive cordon that on this day was lacking one vital ingredient, a line of sight. The thick fog had rendered the defenders blind.

On the left of the 46th Division's line the task of capturing the canal tunnel entrance had been assigned to a special attachment of the 6th North Staffordshire. It was feared that large numbers of the enemy would congregate

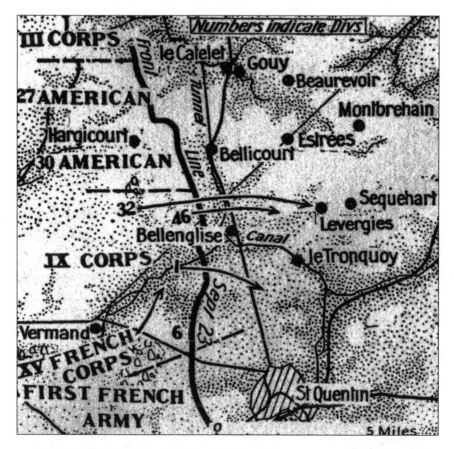

MAP 4 *Proposed British IX Corps attack on the right of the Australians and Americans*

in here and be used to reinforce the German line and threaten the flank of any attacking troops. This detachment would be veering to the north away from the direction of the regiment's main line of advance and would be supported by American troops turning southwards once they were over the tunnel line below Bellicourt. To assist in the capture of these points, two batteries of 18-pounders drawn from the 230 Brigade and 5 Army Brigade, Royal Field Artillery (RFA), were detailed to fire at the tunnel entrances until overtaken by the creeping barrage.[5]

41

The 6th North Staffordshire moved forwards on an 800-yard, two-company front down to the canal. Indirect machine-gun fire spluttered through the fog fired in hope by the Germans opposite. Owing to the fog these machine guns could not be immediately located and silenced. Fortuitously several footbridges were found in tact and these were used by some of the attacking troops to cross the canal. Captain Teeton who had plunged into the icy water and swum across with a line was most unimpressed to emerge and be confronted by dry clad compatriots who had crossed a bridge only a few yards away, it having been invisible in the fog to the now drenched and shivering officer.[6]

Private A. G. Shennan was mortified to find himself as the last man on the left of the battalion's taped start line. He quickly lost touch with his platoon in the fog and, alone, began to cross the main bridge opposite Riqueval Farm. Terrified that it would be blown up at any minute and he with it, he returned to the west side of the canal. Twenty yards south of the footbridge he found his company commander, Captain Humphrey Charlton, preparing to cross through the water. Charlton was amazed to hear the bridge was still standing and led his men back to cross over it. Two Germans were encountered in the process of laying charges to destroy this useful thoroughfare. They were shot and the leads to the charges cut. The explosives were dumped into the canal. About 130 of the enemy were captured, including a battalion commander, shortly after the English troops crossed the bridge.[7] Pressing on quickly past the canal defences to the vicinity of Nigger Copse, the English added a German field gun to their captures. It may have been the same howitzer that the irrepressible Captain Teeton later turned on the enemy.[8]

The 5th South Staffordshire had a slightly larger front of 1,000 yards with each attacking company deployed on a 500-yard front. Owing to the casualties suffered the previous day the support companies were combined into a single entity. No bridges existed in this portion of the canal so the men crossed by using lines and planks. Officers such as 2nd Lieutenant W. B. Brown stood waist deep in the water for nearly an hour pulling men across by hauling lines.

Many groups and individuals became disoriented in the fog. However through the initiative of NCOs such as Corporal A. E. Ferguson, who gathered his own section and other strays together into an assault group, the attack was pressed home close behind the protective barrage line.[9] The troops quickly reached the other side and scrambled up the banks silencing the light machine guns that were firing at them. Here they found the enemy disorganised and surrendering willingly in batches of between fifteen and seventy men. Behind the German infantry a four-gun battery of field guns and its crews was captured while in action on the slopes of the Magny valley near Bullet Copse.

On the right flank of the 46th Division the 6th South Staffordshire Regiment held a short front of 400 yards. They attacked on a single company front in four waves each 100 yards apart. The men waited patiently, crammed tightly together in the congested trenches. Their spirits were buoyed by the magnificent clear night and brightening dawn. When the mist suddenly rolled in their spirits plummeted as the damp grey blanket smothered them. Fearing the worst, they set off at a slow walk with the bullets from their own machine-gun barrage whizzing a few feet above them. About five hundred yards from the canal, as they crossed Chopper ravine, the German counterbarrage fell on them. Guns of all calibres searched blindly for targets in the back areas hoping to disrupt any assembling troops. A few German defenders occupying some trenches set on the downward slope just before the canal were easily overcome.

Reaching the edge of the canal the men stood and peered into the mist. They could not see the other side. Heaving lines and rafts were used to cross as the canal was quite deep in that sector. The water was fetid and stagnant, which made the prospect of an early morning dip even less appealing than it already did to men carrying ninety pounds of equipment above their head while under fire from the embankment opposite. As with the other sectors they crossed quickly and with relative immunity. Some machine guns and bombs were used against them but once the attackers were on their opponents the Germans surrendered freely. Terror-stricken prisoners said they had been cut off without food for twenty-four hours due to the intensity of the barrage. They could do nothing but cower in their dugouts and await their fate.[10] After about two hours the fog gradually began to dissipate and visibility increased to forty yards. Two companies turned to the right and bombed and captured many of the enemy in the cellars and tunnels in Bellenglise as they worked towards linking up with the 1st Division troops in that area.

All along the east bank of the canal large numbers of Germans found themselves trapped in the dugouts as the British infantry swarmed along the embankment. Entrances were quickly barred and the threat of a phosphorus bomb or grenade was enticement enough for most to capitulate. Large amounts of German dead attested to the severity of the supporting barrage. When it opened the din was such that speech was impossible. Some 2,000 nerve-shattered defenders surrendered. Many had been rendered senseless by the noise and concussion of the barrage and were shepherded back towards the rear. As well, the attacking troops were able to report little trouble from the belts of wire that had been effectively cut by the artillery. The ground had been torn to pieces with the trenches and wire blown in all directions.[11]

Still undercover of the fog the leading elements made their way to the first objective line. Some German defenders made good their escape in the fog and smoke. Nevertheless, an hour and forty minutes after zero, the 46th Division was able to report itself over the canal and consolidating for the next phase.

At divisional headquarters the report and confirmation of this astounding success was cause for celebration. Major-General Boyd's day had got off to a cheerful start when he was presented with the latest copy of the *Daily Mail* which had been secured from a motor cyclist just in from Amiens. As the magnitude of the success became known he hurried forwards and was seen crossing the Riqueval bridge with tears of joy running down his cheeks.[12]

The rear echelon area now became a hive of activity as the supporting brigades congregating in Ascension valley swung into motion to leapfrog through the successful assault battalions. Their progress was being hampered somewhat by the hundreds of prisoners being escorted to the rear through the fog. In one case a German officer used his compass to guide his men westward into captivity after losing touch with their escort.[13] Big Bill Wood lying about six hundred yards in rear of the centre of the initial start line had been designated as the prisoner collection point.

The artillerymen were also anxious to get forwards to bring the guns into supporting distance of the next objectives. Here the fog was proving troublesome. Horse teams could not be urged on with any rapidity given that five yards was the maximum distance anybody could see. It would be reckless in the extreme to urge man and beast forwards at the gallop under such conditions.

Another support arm affected by the foggy weather was the trench mortars. Four guns of the 137th Light Trench Mortar Battery had been attached to the 6th South Staffordshire on the right and two to the 6th North Staffordshire on the left. Because of the speed of the advance and limited visibility only one section had been able to get into action. It had silenced a machine gun on the left flank. Given this situation the personnel of the battery were employed as riflemen in the advance.[14]

By 11 a.m. the 137 Brigade was on its objective and reorganising its units, which had become mixed over the course of the morning's fighting. The fog had lifted revealing the magnitude of their triumph. It was time for the supporting brigades to finish the job.

The 138 Brigade, commanded by Lieutenant-Colonel F. G. M. Rowley, formed the left wing of the division and the 139 Brigade, commanded by Lieutenant-Colonel J. Harrington, the right wing. The 4th Leicestershire formed the first wave of the 138 Brigade and was followed by the 5th Lincolnshire which, in turn, was trailed by the 5th Leicestershire Regiment. At 10.15 a.m. the 4th Leicestershire was summoned to go forwards. The supporting brigades had closed up quickly behind the storming brigade. They had orders to go forwards at their discretion to assist the 137 Brigade to fight its way forward if it were held up.[15] This proved unnecessary and they moved ahead in accordance with the artillery timetable. The 4th Leicestershire Regiment reached its start line having suffered only slight casualties during the advance. At 11.20 a.m. it set off towards the next objective undercover of the barrage and with the assistance of four tanks. The Leicesters reached this line quickly and were relieved by the 5th Lincolnshire Regiment at 12.25 p.m.. Little opposition had been encountered. The worst of the men's experience came from shelling as they formed up on the canal.

The 5th Lincolnshire advanced undercover of the barrage with the brigade's allotment of tanks at 12.30 p.m. on the village of Magny la Fosse. Three hundred prisoners and seven guns were captured during the attack on the village. Meanwhile the 5th Leicestershire was forming up on Knobkerry Ridge ready to move through to the objective line east of the village. The appearance of the tanks on the skyline south of Magny la Fosse attracted the attention of the German gunners and brought down unwanted shellfire on the Leicester's right flank. The men scrambled into the shelter of the old trenches until it was time to resume their advance. Setting off again at 1.40 p.m. they were on their objective by 2.30 p.m.. Some of the men could not be restrained from trying to run through the support barrage to attack a battery of German guns that had unlimbered near the old Merville mill and was firing point blank into their line. One or two men were lost in the dash but the battery was scattered and the guns left on the field. The Leicester's immediately set about consolidating their position and patrolling their flanks to gain touch with the troops on both their left and right. This was achieved by 3 p.m.[16]

Scattered along the slopes over which the British had advanced lay the hulks of ten tanks in various states of ruin. The 138 Brigade was still under fire from German guns firing obliquely from Levergies and Le Tronquoy to its right. The 139 Brigade had yet to come up to cover their exposed flank. To make matters worse the headquarters of the Leicesters was strafed by one of its own planes. Adding to this series of unhappy circumstances was the death of the 5th Leceisters' padre the Reverend C. B. W. Buck. Buck had led a platoon of D Company into position along with some of the headquarter details on his way up to the line. Now, in the act of attempting to rescue some injured tank men, he was killed by a shell.[17]

On the right the advance of the 139 Brigade had lagged slightly behind its neighbour. German guns in the vicinity of Lehaucourt were enfilading its right flank as it pushed forwards. The right flank battalion was the 6th Sherwood Foresters and its commander was the *Boy's Own* Lieutenant-Colonel The Reverend B. W. Vann who had originally applied to become an army chaplain but grew impatient and took a combatant commission instead. Already wounded six times in the war, awarded the Military Cross and bar as well as a Croix de Guerre, he was now about to add a Victoria Cross to his ribbon set. After settling his men down under the bothersome fire he dashed towards the village with some of them, singularly killing five German gunners as the artillerymen attempted to bring their horses up to remove the guns.[18]

By day's end the 32nd British Division had leapfrogged the victorious 46th Division and reached the army's objective for the day on the Lehaucourt Ridge. On this high ground a mounted German officer tried vainly to rally his men but both rider and horse were shot down. The 79th German Reserve Division, charged with defending the sector, had been completely routed.[19]

The magnitude of the day's success was considered by a trooper of the 2nd Life Guards as being 'unheard of at the time'.[20] It was certainly unexpected and the great elation felt by all was magnified by the general expectation that the position could not be carried. Spirits were soaring and the gunners and drivers of the 168 Brigade, RFA, were addressed by their commanding officer at the close of the day and told that they 'were winning the war'.[21]

CHAPTER FOUR

American 30th Division

'Our men expose themselves unnecessarily.' – American officer

In the predawn of 29 September, Major-General E. M. Lewis' American 30th Division lay on its designated taped lines waiting for the support barrage to begin. The division's nickname was 'Old Hickory' in affection for the former American president and Tennessean, Andrew Jackson. These national guardsmen were drawn from the Carolinas and Tennessee though their commanding general was a native of New Albany, Indiana. Behind the waiting infantry along the whole Australian–American–British front the artillery stood almost wheel to wheel. For days the guns had been sending shells crashing down on the Hindenburg Line unremittingly. Sweating gunners stripped to the waist and blackened by grime worked furiously at their guns cheered on by the passing infantry. Silent batteries that had lain idle through the previous bombardments were now adding their weight to the murderous inferno.[1]

Men from the leading 60 Brigade peered anxiously ahead of them unable to see anything through the fog and drifting smoke of the barrage. The division's machine guns were chattering away raining a hail of bullets on the German lines. The German counterbarrage opened in reply. It was not particularly heavy but it was well placed and caused a number of casualties among the supporting troops forming behind the American jump-off position.

The 60 Brigade, consisting of two regiments, formed the division's front line. The 119th Regiment was on the left and the 120th Regiment on the right. One company of the 120th with a section of machine guns attached was assigned to the capture of the tunnel entrance at Riqueval in conjunction with the British on their flank. Each regiment had two battalions in the front line with the third in support charged with mopping up any pockets of resistance passed over in the initial advance. The concept of mopping up had been thoroughly stressed by General Monash in the prebattle plans and was undoubtedly reinforced by the Australian officers attached to the American units. It was a factor that would loom large in postwar evaluations of the battle and conduct of the American troops.

The 59 Brigade comprising the American 117th and 118th Regiments formed the divisional reserve. They lay on their taped lines, which had been put down during the night by the American 105th Engineers – white tape stretched on the ground and was tenuously held by clods of earth.[2] The 117th Regiment was to cross the tunnel and face south to form a defensive flank for the division. Given Monash's lack of faith in any likely success of the 46th Division, the role of the 117th was potentially a critical one in the overall corps plan.

Opposing the Americans were two divisions of the German 51st Corps. The 185th Division held the northern sector with three regiments: the 161st Regiment occupied the line below Quennemont Farm; the 28th Regiment defended the trench line west of Bellicourt; and the 65th Regiment south of that. Three regiments of the 75th Reserve Division stretched from the left of its neighbouring division south past the tunnel's southern entrant into the British IX Corps front. From north to south they were the 251st, 250th and 249th Regiments. Each divisional sector had at least half a dozen tank forts crammed with field guns, heavy and light machine guns and anti-tank rifles. As well, sections of 'close fighting batteries' were placed in support of the infantry. These were especially situated to deal with any armoured penetration and proved immensely successful over the course of the battle.[3]

At zero hour the Americans disappeared into the mist and groped their way forwards. The barrage was so loud they had to yell to be heard a foot away.[4] Some lost the barrage in the fog and strayed into it – an unfortunate occurrence that caused unnecessary casualties. The infantry was joined by thirty-four Mark V tanks from the 1st Tank Battalion. Twelve (A Company) were assigned to the 119th Regiment on the left. A composite company of ten tanks was assigned to the 120th on the right and twelve (B Company) to the 117th in support. An infantryman was placed with each tank to act as a guide for the crew inside. The exercise was somewhat problematic given that one end of the tank could not be seen from the other in the fog. The drivers of the tanks could not see the ground over which they had to pass. Nevertheless those infantrymen who were able to stick with a tank benefited from pathways being crushed through the wire and from machine-gun nests being routed or destroyed by the metal behemoths.

Overall though the presence of the tanks had not been as decisive as had been hoped. On the left, one broke a track before it reached the jump-off line while three others were ditched behind the line as they made their way forwards over badly broken ground. Of those that went forwards five were ditched just west of the German line. Two managed to cross the tunnel line before one of them was knocked out. Another – from A Company, 1st Tank Battalion – reached the Green Line and moved 600 yards beyond to a point near a sunken road at Bank Copse where it too was knocked out. This tank was spotted by British planes and contributed to the impression that the Americans had made good on the Green Line.[5]

On the right the tanks were a few minutes behind the infantry at zero. The absence of the tanks in the initial advance was certainly an inconvenience for the 120th Regiment on whose front the wire had not been destroyed to the same degree as in other sub-sectors. Nevertheless all tanks from the composite company eventually reached the vicinity of the tunnel and Bellicourt but none was able to reach the Green Line. Three suffered direct hits, two being burnt out and the other ditched. Another was immobilised when it threw a track. In all only four of these were able to make it back to their rallying point.

The tanks that went forwards with the reserve, the 117th Regiment, fared better. They had been waiting for an hour on the start line for the infantry to arrive. When the infantry was up, the fog and smoke which was being carried back by a slight southeasterly breeze made concerted action difficult. With the assistance of two section commanders, Major Miskin, the company commander, was able to shepherd his machines forwards by degrees. Eventually five of these tanks arrived on the Green Line where they did good work with British troops already working east of Bellicourt and north of Nauroy. Seven of this dozen-strong company eventually rallied after the attack.[6]

One downside of the tanks' involvement was that they frequently broke the telephone lines which were laid along the ground, thus making communication with front and rear less reliable. These lines were already prone to frequent breaks from the artillery shells that deluged the battlefield.[7] Wireless communication served as a secondary source but was not as instantaneous due to the need to encode and decode messages sent and received.

The fog though proved the most limiting factor in the tanks' performance. Although considerably minimising the likelihood of casualties to the tanks and crew it also diminished their fighting prowess. Unable to see, the tanks were unable to fire selectively. Only 30,000 rounds of small-arms ammunition were fired and fewer than 300 rounds from the six-pounder armament. Seven tanks in fact did not fire a single shot. It was estimated that about twenty to thirty machine-gun posts were accounted for. Beyond that, the tank men contented themselves with the knowledge that they had played with obvious effect on the enemy whenever they hove into sight.[8]

The heavy mist also played havoc with the infantry formations. Attacking regiments became disorganised after only a few hundred yards and the assault broke up into a series of disconnected small groups fighting their way forwards. Where tanks were found they were used with good effect to blot out machine-gun and *minenwerfer* posts. Some had penetrated behind the headquarters of the 28th Regiment which was holding the sector of Le Catelet–Nauroy Line directly east of Bellicourt. The commander of its second battalion, Count Wolff-Metternich, was killed while trying to defend his position with some of his runners.[9]

By mid-morning the American 120th Regiment had captured a portion of the tunnel line. They had suffered some casualties in the supporting barrage, some of the men having strayed into it, as they picked their way through the wire strung thickly across their front. Once clear, they managed to push through the area between the town of Bellicourt and the southern tunnel entrant.[10] One party of three or four men under Captain Thomas Byrd of G Company actually passed over Railway Ridge and thus through Le Catelet–Nauroy Line to the Green Line objective. They remained on this position for about twenty minutes without contact with any other Americans before withdrawing back to the Hindenburg Line. While on the objective two British planes flew low over their position. These men, seen through a break in the fog, may have been the Americans reported by the reconnaissance mission as being on the Green Line. If so, their brief visitation assumed significance far beyond their actual tactical effect.

On his return Byrd led some of the 120th Regiment forwards again, mopping up trenches southeast of Bellicourt and pushing forwards up the Bellicourt–Nauroy Road. Along the road he was joined by Major J. A. Graham and a mixed party of the 2nd Battalion, 120th Regiment.[11] Heavy machine-gun fire from Nauroy however held up any further advance. This hardy group of Americans inched forwards up the main communication trench from Bellicourt and drew up a ragged line at the base of the slopes leading up to Nauroy.[12] The Germans responded to the pressure on this part of their line by dispatching two sections of field guns from the 55th Artillery Regiment to Nauroy and the woods north of the town to strengthen this portion of the 75th Reserve Division's front.[13]

On the left the American 119th Regiment was struggling. Fire from the direction of Malakoff Wood and Quennemont Farm in the 27th Division sector forced them to refuse their left flank. North of Bellicourt though they managed to cross the tunnel mound towards the railway embankment before being arrested by fire from Cabaret Wood and the trenches in that vicinity. Here the German infantry from the 161st Regiment had been reinforced by two companies of engineers.[14]

The Americans of the 119th Regiment were strung out diagonally across the front. Their right was linked with the 120th Regiment before Le Catelet–Nauroy Line with their left resting back on the tunnel line where they were joined with some groups of the 108th Regiment. Major F. E. Hotblack, alert to the problems of the enfilading fire in this sector, took two tanks of the 16th Battalion (then being held in reserve) and drove up the ridge to try and suppress the troublesome fire. He overran a number of machine-gun posts before both tanks were knocked out. During the course of the fighting he was wounded in the head, his fourth wound of the war. Although partially blinded he managed to hold on to the position, gained with a handful of his men, by using captured German weapons until reinforced a few hours later.[15]

The reported American success was something of a mirage. The Green Line had not been gained and the village of Nauroy was still in German possession. Throughout the morning 30th Division headquarters had received no information that caused any great alarm about the success of the operation. It was not until the Australian 5th Division arrived behind them that it became apparent that all was not unfolding as smoothly as first thought. The Australians were anxious to determine what was happening in their immediate front as they had expected a clear run to their jump-off position. It was the reports of these incoming units that began to crystallise the situation in the minds of the 30th Division headquarter staff.

The 117th Regiment was one unit that had disappeared into the fog. Telephone communication with the regiment had been lost either through the

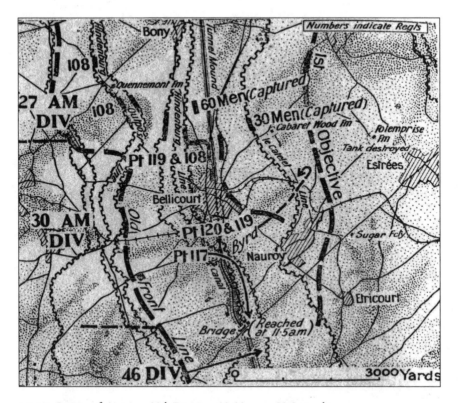

MAP 5 *Position of American 30th Division, 10.30 a.m., 29 September*

wire being cut by shell fire or run over by the tanks. Divisonal HQ had not heard from the 117th since the previous evening and was frantically trying to establish a line of communication. A messenger was sent to the regiment at 6.30 a.m. asking for information. On arrival the runner also tried to organise the repair or re-establishment of a telephone wire to restore communications. Some of the 117th Regiment ended up mixed with the 120th Regiment near Bellicourt.[16]

Compounding the problem was the effect of a smoke screen that was put down at 8.32 a.m. by No. 4 Special Company of the Royal Engineers. This screen was to mask the American's movement south where they were to clear the Germans along the east bank near the tunnel entrant. Combined with the natural fog it served to befuddle most of the troops in it. A large portion of the 117th would be picked up by the Australians marching onto the field. Captain George A. Blair however did not lose his sense of direction and with men from his C Company and strays from the 119th and 120th Regiments he moved down the east side of the canal, clearing dugouts, while firing across the water at the Germans still lodged on the other side. He captured a number of Germans before linking with the British troops who had forced their way over the canal. This was at about 11.10 a.m.[17]

The advance of the 30th Division's left flank was hopelessly compromised by the problems that had visited the 27th Division attack where the German defence of Bony was proving obstinate. Pockets of German defenders from a company of the 251st Regiment were still defending Bellicourt. Other isolated parties held fragments of the front line above the town. The latter were considered to have sifted down from the north through the 27th Division's front to reinforce those areas after the majority of the 30th Division's attacking line had passed by.[18]

The popular claim made at the time and subsequently is that the Americans had failed to mop up adequately, that they had rushed forwards in their raw enthusiasm and paid little heed to the vital act of ensuring German defenders were not left active in their wake. This was a view that Monash happily ascribed to in his postwar accounts as it made a convenient scapegoat of the Americans for the difficulties that engulfed the supporting Australian divisions. The reality is that the German defences were heavily occupied and that the subsequent advancing lines had little opportunity to mop up as they became embroiled in major firefights of their own.

The myth of the tunnel also permeates through many accounts with descriptions of the Germans appearing out of secret hideaways and passageways to wreak havoc on the rear and flanks of troops that had passed over them. Such views do a disservice to the American endeavour on both divisional fronts and fail to come to grips, except in the most superficial way, with the problems faced. Examination of the tunnel after the battle revealed it to be virtually uninhabitable. The atmosphere was described by the Germans as 'fuggy'. There is no evidence to suggest it had acted as a major thoroughfare or concentration point for German reinforcements.[19] Isolated bands sought refuge in it during the bombardments but for the most part it was unused and the most likely safety zones for the defenders were the dugouts burrowed and cemented into the spoil on top of the tunnel.

Australia's official war historian, C. E. W. Bean, did not believe the tunnel constituted a vital underground marshalling point in the German defence. He concluded that the Americans had not rushed forward impetuously and that the chief resistance had not come from bypassed Germans or those sent rearward but from 'supports and reserves attacking normally from the front'. He believed that the Americans had been set too difficult a task for inexperienced troops.[20] A few days after the battle Major W. F. L Hartigan submitted his observations of the fighting and, while acknowledging many of the shortfalls in the American performance, was of the opinion that 'seasoned troops' confronted by the combination of the smoke barrage and heavy fog 'would not have known where to mop'.[21]

Without doubt the fog provided the first major hurdle that the Americans had to overcome. Unlike the British on their right, the doughboys did not have a tangible terrain feature such as the open canal (once found) from which to take a bearing. The fact that the German defences were located virtually on that same line made the 46th Division's job of striking at their targets a far easier task. The Americans had to pick their way through masses of wire which on the 30th Division front had not been completely destroyed and which had to be confronted, at some points, without the aid of the tanks which were late in arriving.

In the thick fog German defenders were easily missed especially by units that had become quickly disorganised. Casualties among the advancing Americans were high and this was especially felt in the officers' ranks. An inherent problem in the American divisions was the absence of suitably trained officers and their inexperience led to unnecessary casualties. As a consequence many groups of American troops found themselves without leaders and this had a marked and varied affect on their ability to operate. Some pushed on while others lost their initiative completely. The net effect of fog, American inexperience and German resolve meant that only incomplete gains had been made by the 30th Division.

At 12.50 p.m. Colonel Tyson, commanding the 117th Regiment, was ordered to send his reserve battalion to Bellicourt to mop it up and then push on to the northeast and assist the 119th Regiment, which was struggling to get forward due to opposition emanating from the 27th Division front around Bony. These were all places that the Americans had earlier believed to be in their clean possession. Lieutenant-Colonel McCrosky was sent from Division HQ to assume command of the situation in Bellicourt.[22]

Brigadier-General Iven Mackay, who was commanding the section of the Australian mission attached to 30th Division, immediately went forward to assist on learning of the failure of the 27th Division and of the disorganisation of the 30th Division. Mackay wrote down a series of instructions for General Lewis in regard to the reorganising and controlling of units and employment of staffs. He arranged for these instructions to be set in train in the rear echelons and at divisional headquarters. He then went forward to the headquarters of the attacking 59 and 60 Brigades to instruct the commanders of those units. Later in the afternoon, Mackay accompanied General Lewis to Headquarters Australian 5th Division to arrange details for the withdrawal of the Americans.[23]

The extent of the 30th Division's disorganisation was borne out in Major W. F. L. Hartigan's report to G-3, the Americans' operations branch of staff. Assembly points for stragglers were unknown, and stragglers in large numbers

58

clogged the division's rear. Hartigan personally assembled and directed five hundred strays back to the front. Men bringing in prisoners singly rather than in groups, men escorting wounded comrades, and others seeking attention for superficial injuries such as backs hurt from falling in shell holes, all contributed to the congestion. Inhibiting the efficient management of the problem was a lack of training and initiative on the part of the American NCOs. Many did not have compasses – a reflection of the supply problems and shortages that afflicted the AEF generally – and this caused the mist and smoke that limited visibility in the early phase of the battle to be doubly blinding. Men separated from their own units exhibited a marked disinclination to join others or to form new temporary squads to move the battle forwards. This attitude also precluded any willingness to assume higher command responsibilities in the face of missing or disabled officers. The American advance was further compromised by a lack of understanding on the part of company officers and NCOs about their unit's objectives and mission.[24] Many of the problems were the same as had afflicted the untested Australians at Gallipoli and were symptomatic of green troops and staffs in battle. An American officer stated, in relation to the training of the 30th Division, that it was 'very apparent that our men expose themselves unnecessarily and do not hug the folds of the ground or crawl as they should'.[25] That the 30th Division got as far forward as they did in the face of such inexperience is perhaps testament to the men's exuberance and desire to succeed.

The battle would ultimately claim 3,146 killed and wounded in the division.[26] The numbers of casualties sustained was certainly excessive and prompted comment from many incoming Australians. One staff officer in the 32nd Battalion thought the American reverse had a sobering effect as 'it stopped them telling us any more that they had come over to finish off the war for us'.[27] More sympathetically Lieutenant-Colonel Sloan of the 30th Battalion looked on the grim harvest of American dead as something reminiscent of the slaughter of Australians at Fromelles two years earlier.[28]

Captain T. C. Barbour of the same unit believed the aftermath of the frightful slaughter that he witnessed was indicative of a sanguinary engagement that, despite the evident failure of the Americans to gain their objectives fully, was proof of a wonderful fight on their part. Barbour believed that Bellicourt would stand as a perpetual monument to the Americans who had perished there. His observations also took in what he considered the obstinate nature of the German resistance. He counted numerous posts where German machine gunners had died at their guns. More unusual in his view was the finding of *minenwerfer* crews bayoneted at their posts. These men he claimed were usually the first to clear out during an enemy advance. The thick fog had undoubtedly allowed the Americans in many cases to get to close grips with their enemy. Perhaps the starkest image of the fierceness of the combat was the gruesome spectacle of a German and American soldier huddled on the ground each impaled by the other's bayonet.[29]

The 30th Division line as it existed when the 5th Division came on its straggling rear cannot be cited with any exactness. It lay roughly on a line east of Cabaret Wood Farm passing south, paralleling Le Catelet–Nauroy line to the western slopes of Nauroy. There, in the trenches, small and intermingled groups of the 117th, 119th and 120th Regiments clung steadfastly to their gains largely unaware of the confusion behind them.

CHAPTER FIVE

American 27th Division

'*A serious complication*' — C. E. W. Bean

The disastrous outcome of the preliminary operation had rattled the confidence of the New York state guard division. Their trepidation towards the forthcoming attack was completely warranted. As previously noted compensation for the lack of artillery cover was provided through the provision of extra tanks on the 27th Division front. Twenty-three tanks of the American 301st Tank Battalion had been allocated to the division. This battalion consisted of British tanks manned by American crews and was distributed through the attacking companies.

The plan of the 27th Division on 29 September was to get forwards as quickly as they could to catch the main barrage and move onto the Green Line east of Guoy. The 54 Brigade was to make the attack with the 107th Regiment on the left and 108th Regiment on the right. Each regiment would attack on a two-battalion front with one battalion in reserve. The 53 Brigade formed the reserve. The 105th Regiment was detailed to follow the left of the 107th Regiment over the canal and to turn northwards to outflank the Germans holding the tunnel's northern entrant at Vendhuille. The 106th Regiment, which had been badly used up in the preliminary operation, was combined into a single battalion to mop up behind the right battalion of the 107th Regiment. The 18th Division of the British III Corps would advance on Vendhuille in support of the 27th Division's left flank. The 27th Division planned to be on the Green Line at 11 a.m. at which time the Australian 3rd Division would pass through them to attack the Red Line.

Sergeant Merritt D. Cutler of I Company, 107th Regiment, remembered getting little sleep and being roused at 2.30 a.m. to get ready for the attack. He appreciated a big half tumbler of rum dolled out to the men by the British prior to the attack.[1] At midnight those not on other duties were fed a hot meal of stew with bread. Men engaged in much cheerful kidding to mask their natural nervousness.[2] Uppermost in Cutler's mind was the thought of not wanting to look 'yellow' to the men around him. He was shot in the leg during the advance but continued on oblivious to his wound until his attention was drawn to his blood-saturated leg later in the afternoon.[3]

Prior to the infantry attack, six tanks from the 4th Tank Battalion made an unsupported sortie towards the German line to 'mop up' ground not captured in the previous attack. Working forward in pairs ten minutes before zero they reported suppressing two machine guns at Gillemont Farm, meeting no opposition at the Knoll and finding Quennemont Farm clear. Two of the tanks ran into the old British minefield on the outward journey as did three others on their return. Bean suggested this excursion did little more than alert the Germans to the forthcoming attack.[4] More critically though the extraordinary discovery that the Knoll and Quennemont Farm were largely devoid of defenders at this early hour makes the return of the tanks an almost culpable act. Knowing the main attack was soon to begin and knowing the devastation that had been wrought on the Americans traversing that fire-swept slope the previous days, surely the tanks should have tried to remain near those positions.

When the main barrage opened at 5.50 a.m. both the leading regiments got off to a good start. They advanced nonchalantly with their rifles slung across their shoulders and smoking cigarettes. Above them crackled their own machine-gun barrage and before them spat the venomous retaliation of their enemy. Sheaths of German SOS flares immediately rocketed skywards to alert their gunners and call in the counterbarrage. Fortunately for the doughboys, the German response passed over the main attacking lines and fell into the rear area causing only a few casualties.[5]

On the extreme right, the 2nd Battalion, 108th Regiment struck trouble from advanced machine-gun nests around the Malakoff Farm vicinity. These were outflanked and suppressed with grenade and rifle fire.[6] Just after 8 a.m. this battalion was reported as being northeast of Quennemont Farm astride the Dirk valley road heading into Bony. Indeed a later report stated that elements of the brigade had entered Bony in good order an hour and a half earlier. The 2nd Battalion, 108th Regiment met heavy opposition at Quennemont Farm. Finding it impossible to move directly against this strongpoint the battalion attempted to bypass it. North of the farm the left companies of the defending 90th Regiment were forced back. Greater success was achieved south of the farm where the 56th Regiment was driven out of the outpost line.[7] Moving on towards Bony the Americans entered the Hindenburg Line south of the town. Here with a force of approximately two hundred men they maintained their position, fighting up the trenches towards Bony and beating off a number of counterattacks. All this was achieved with numerous prisoners needing to be kept subjugated in their midst. They also found touch with the American 119th Regiment on the left of the 30th Division's front.

At 9.10 a.m. the 3rd Battalion, 108th Regiment operating on the left reported suffering casualties from machine guns firing from Gillemont Farm. This battalion could make no headway and suffered heavily. One portion of it did manage to move south of the farm into Claymore valley where it was halted by fire from Bony. The survivors took cover in a sunken road west of the town.[8] Despite these losses others continued pushing on to the canal tunnel line. An hour later Australian officers, lieutenant-colonels Crowther and Salisbury, went forwards to ascertain the situation of the doughboys in this sector. They were able confidently to say, after interrogating prisoners, the Americans were on the tunnel position at 10.15 a.m.[9]

The supporting 1st Battalion, 108th Regiment had also been under heavy fire from the outset. It advanced only 400 yards in which position it remained while fighting raged ahead of it.[10] The Battalion was able to mop up some machine-gun nests but the majority of its work appears to have been spent gathering up disoriented Germans and providing assistance in escorting rearward those prisoners being brought back from the front.[11]

The heavy fire received from Gillemont Farm was a portent of worse things to come on the left of the line. On the Knoll, which had proved so troublesome in the previous days, the Germans were again present in strength. As well, machine-gun and anti-tank fire was raking the approach through the natural corridors that passed southeast of the Knoll (Macquincourt valley) and Gillemont Farm (Claymore valley).

The American 107th Regiment advanced between the British on its left and the 108th Regiment on its right. For the attack, the battalions formed on two-company fronts in two lines fifty yards apart. Skirmish order was adopted with a five-pace gap between each man and the platoons in two lines twenty yards between them. The NCOs had been told that the success of the assault lay largely in their hands as they were to be engaged in a squad leaders' fight. Prior to the attack they plied the Australian sergeants attached to the battalion with questions and were as ready as was humanly possible given all the circumstances.[12]

On the right the 3rd Battalion, 107th Regiment was slowed by fire on its flank from Gillemont Farm and from Lone Tree Trench in its front where the German 27th Regiment was holding on desperately. This trench line effectively connected Gillemont Farm with the Knoll to the north. West of it ran Willow Trench which the Americans successfully carried, clawing through the wire with the barbs tearing at their coats and leggings, before becoming pinned down between it and Lone Tree Trench. At one stage gas masks were donned in response to smoke drifting across this position.[13]

The 3rd Battalion, 107th Regiment had been spared significant casualties until it began its descent into the valley against the German line. The left of the line particularly came under heavy attack as they moved towards Gillemont Farm. Captain Claude Leland, walking stick in hand, led his men forwards. With him was Captain George B. Bradish of K Company. Leland strode forwards while Bradish left him to go in search of some trench mortars. The Lewis gun squad with them had lost most of its carriers and one of the gunners, Private Tuthill, staggered forwards with the gun slung across his shoulder while carrying a bucket of ammunition pans. At Willow Trench he cleared the way by firing his Lewis gun from the hip while Leland fired off rounds from his pistol.[14]

In another display of initiative in what proved a sacrificial act, Little Barker – belonging to one of the Lewis gun squads – crouched on the edge of a shell hole so that his No. 1 could rest the gun on his shoulder to gain a better line of sight. Barker was killed and the gunner wounded. Undeterred the Americans crawled up to the German trenches and showered them with Mills grenades before attacking some of the dugouts. They then had to endure a determined counterattack by the Germans but succeeded in driving it back from whence it had come.[15]

The losses sustained by the battalion's intelligence section are an indication of the severity of casualties suffered throughout the battalion. Of these twenty specialists, six were killed and ten wounded – a 75 per cent casualty rate.[16] Merritt Cutler remembered the ranks getting thinner and thinner and the men going down 'like pins in a bowling alley'.[17]

Captain Bradish's search for mortars proved fruitless. Instead he came across some tanks attached to the incoming Australian 10 Brigade. He explained the situation to the tank officers who decided that their duty lay in clearing the way forwards. Guided by Bradish and some stragglers from his command, they advanced on Gillemont Farm. At about 11.30 a.m. an abortive effort was made against the farm. Tank after tank was hit and one ran up against the old British minefield adding to the escalating number of wrecks there. Bradish's men were driven back and he eventually made his way forwards again to Willow Trench with a reinforcing company from the 105th Regiment.[18]

Meanwhile Captain Leland had become separated from his men when he tried to find reinforcements. He recorded seeing a German plane operating about a hundred yards behind him on the northern outskirt of Gillemont Farm. The plane attracted the attention of many on the ground at the time. Lewis gunners of the incoming Australian 40th Battalion fired on a German plane of the 'red devil' variety and saw, either through their own handiwork or from others blazing away, the stricken plane spiral to the ground.[19] Its fate led Leland to presume that friendly troops lay west of his position.[20]

Leland had been in Grub Lane where he had run into a band of Germans before beating a hasty retreat. His withdrawal took him south towards the Bony road. Looking down at Bony through field glasses provided by a German captured in his travels, he could see nothing but the carnage and wreckage left in the wake of the early morning battle. There was no indication of any friendly line established at Bony although an American flag pinned to the ground alongside a trench was proof that there had been one.[21]

Further to the left 1st Battalion, 107th Regiment met with an equivalent wall of machine-gun fire. It managed to gain a section of Knoll Trench and Willow Trench south of the Knoll. Attempts to push into the Macquincourt valley were met with a deadly metal rain from machine guns from the ridges ahead of them. The 27th Division machine guns were contacted to sweep these positions but they did not succeed in silencing them. Some tanks that came forwards to aid the infantry were also lost to the lethal fire. As with the troops on their right some elements of this battalion did get through to the Hindenburg Line.[22]

A liaison force drawn from the British 54 Brigade of the 18th Division had been assigned the task of accompanying the advance of the 107th Regiment along the south side of the Macquincourt valley. Its principal role was to assume a position astride the canal below Vendhuille keeping it under observation with the hope of preventing the destruction of the bridges there. This force comprised two companies of the 2nd Bedfordshire Regiment, B Company of the 18th Battalion Machine Gun Corps and the 80th Field Company, Royal Engineers. It was commanded by Major Patterson of the machine-gun company. Should the American attack succeed the 18th Division was to then proceed to the second stage of its operation by mopping up Vendhuille and preparing the way for the rest of the III Corps.[23]

The British had waited for the Americans to get forwards before they advanced in support. Aware of the absence of a supporting artillery barrage the liaison force was reticent to expose its own flank.[24] The right of this group had established a line along a portion of Knoll Switch northeast of the Knoll itself. There they became intermixed with elements of the two American supporting battalions, 1st Battalion, 105th Regiment and 3rd Battalion, 105th Regiment, which had borne off to the left in the smoke and fog. Into this mix was added Company M of the 106th Regiment, which had been led forwards by Major Buckley through the mist. With patrols pushing forwards to feel out the enemy positions and using compasses to gain their bearings they had advanced by a series of rushes. All around them was a scene of desolation. The mangled corpses of the dead of the previous and current battle were littered among the debris left by the barrage. The earth was torn and trenches demolished. Broken equipment lay all over the ground, which was crossed by acres of barbed wire. Amongst this carnage and debris was found the body of Lieutenant Turner and others killed in the fight of 27 September. Here, along the summit of the hill, Buckley's company dug in with the British on their left. The support company had become the front line.[25]

Somewhere to the right of Buckley's troops, Captain Henry Maslin led 1st Battalion, 105th Regiment through the fog down a sunken road and got forward of the Knoll. Through the mist his men could see remnants of the German 84th Regiment in trenches behind them. They turned back and attacked these troops capturing the majority. Some of the defenders fell back towards the main Hindenburg Line. Believing the 107th Regiment to be ahead of him, Maslin led his men, according to his testimony, due east for about a mile. He moved down the Macquincourt valley until he came up flush against the Hindenburg Line. As German opposition thickened he withdrew back to the vicinity of the Knoll position where the 3rd Battalion, 105th Regiment had formed a defensive line.[26]

The Knoll position was reported as being captured at 9 a.m. It is difficult to assess whether this was in fact the case – the fate of later units coming up against it suggest that it was not seized in its entirety. Maslin and his men may have captured some but not necessarily all of the German defenders there. Certainly, if some Germans had hung on here, they became increasingly isolated as British and American troops seized the trenches north, east and south of the position. The belief that the position had succumbed may have been fostered by the fact that hardy bands of Americans and the British on the left managed to pass around it and gain some of the ground to the west between the Knoll and the main German line. However pushing into the Macquincourt valley between the Knoll and Gillemont Farm these groups – Maslin's being one of them – met with heavy machine-gun fire from Macquincourt Trench, 500 yards southwest of Vendhuille, and from Macquincourt Farm directly in their front. The Germans had a number of tank forts in this area, set on the slopes behind Macquincourt Trench extending southwards. One of these accounted for seven tanks. One however was captured by a party of Americans and used as a strong post behind German lines until abandoned at nightfall.[27] It is difficult to establish exactly when these actions took place but it was most likely some time between 8.20 a.m. and 9 a.m.

Some of 1st Battalion, 105th Regiment had followed the 3rd Battalion, 105th Regiment into the British sector. Other elements were held up by the heavy fire coming from the Knoll. To the south the 2nd Battalion, 108th Regiment was similarly broken up by fire from this position but, taking cover in shell holes and trenches, was able to maintain a defensive position. One section of the battalion found itself in Willow Trench where it barricaded approaches to prevent the further advance of the Germans – it being noted that they were filtering over the Macquincourt valley ridge into Lone Tree Trench paralleling the American line.[28]

The Americans had been able to advance slightly further south through Claymore valley and Dirk valley to reach the Hindenburg Line. Reports from a wounded lieutenant and from Major Gillet of the 106th Regiment, who had been wounded in the arm, placed the leading elements of the Americans in this part of the line by 9 a.m. but with the ominous observation that heavy machine-gun fire was emanating from trenches that had been passed over.[29]

Lieutenant W. O. Pasefield of the Australian 11 Field Artillery Brigade had been assigned to the 3rd Battalion, 105th Regiment as its artillery liaison officer. Unable to get a runner to this battalion he moved forwards in search of them. His journey saw him catch up with the 107th Regiment as they were passing Gillemont Farm. He followed a body of about a hundred Americans – probably the 3rd Battalion, 107th Regiment – who were rushing forward in small groups charging machine-gun posts with fixed bayonets – it being possible to get close enough to do so under cover of the fog. One witness to a bayonet fight was Private Raymond R. Williams, H Company, 107th Regiment. He remembered the yell of one German driven through with a bayonet as being so chilling that it rose above the noise of battle and caused everybody to stand still with bated breath.[30]

This group of the 107th Regiment passed through the Hindenburg Line about 8 a.m. and became lost to Pasefield's view after they crossed over or around the high ground known as the Knob and down the slopes into the Lauban valley across which Le Catelot–Nauroy Line ran southwards from Guoy. Pasefield observed that the wire had been well cut in this vicinity and that little artillery fire was being brought to bear on the area between 9 a.m. and 10.30 a.m. The artilleryman noted large numbers of American dead but few German casualties. He also observed that many enemy machine-gun posts were well concealed in the tall weeds east of the Torrens Canal, which ran through Le Catelet and Guoy. His concern was that these had been passed and not mopped up and he claimed on his return to have met many Americans who said they had no orders to mop up.

Far from being an indictment on the American method of attack, such statements actually reflected the tactic practised through the British Army that the first waves did not mop up and that this was a job left to the subsequent lines. What was evident from the Australian's journey was that few Americans had got through the Hindenburg Line onto the morning's objectives and that the bulk of the attacking force had been brought to a halt against the old outpost line. A group of ten men from the 105th Regiment, which Pasefield found sheltered in shell holes west of the Knoll, claimed that they had actually gained their objectives but had been told to retire. Pasefield's observations reveal that many of the detachments he came across had become lost and disconnected from their units.[31]

Australia's official war historian concluded that Pasefield was probably mistaken in his observations. Bean based his conclusion on the fact that no American troops were mentioned in the area Pasefield described in any of the German unit histories that the historian had subsequently examined. However given the combination of reports from the air – of claims by American soldiers that the Hindenburg Line had been breached, of interviews by experienced officers with prisoners – and given the detail in Pasefield's report and of the inexact nature of many unit histories it is conceivable that the Australian artillery observer's account might indeed have been true. Lieutenant McIntyre of the 107th Regiment, repatriated from Germany in December 1918, claimed he was captured between the Hindenburg Line and canal below Guoy at about 7.15 a.m.[32] He and his orderly, Private William J. Cairns, certainly appeared to have been captured while fighting behind the main German line.[33]

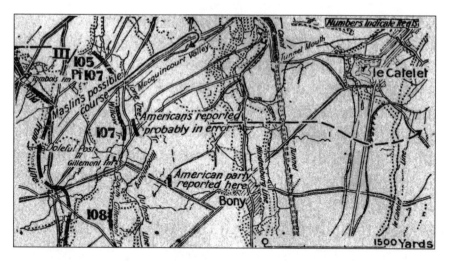

MAP 6 *Position of American 27th Division, 10 a.m., 29 September*

The tendency of most troops and commanders assessing the enemy resistance was to attribute it to a failure to mop up. Because the need to mop up had been so pointedly driven home in the prebattle discussions it was undoubtedly uppermost in everyone's mind as the most likely danger and thus the most likely explanation for failure when failure came. That fact also suggests that its importance would hardly have been forgotten even by the greenest troops and their officers. The heavy resistance being brought to bear against the American flank and rear sprang from the vigorous commitment of the Germans to the principle of the counterattack that governed their defensive policy. Available troops were being fed into the fight as quickly as possible at the most threatened points. In addition, the reserve divisions – the 121st Alsatian and 185th Prussian – had been summoned early in the morning when it was realised that a major assault was underway. Throughout the day the German reinforcements in the sector came from reserve companies placed within and behind the main line.

The retirement of the Americans on the left forced a change of front on the British liaison force. Colonel Guy Blewitt who had ridden forwards on his horse to survey the situation quickly dismounted and, with a rifle in hand, began organising a defensive flank to face southwards towards the Gillemont spur against which the Germans were counterattacking in force. He hurried off a message to inform the advancing Australian 3rd Division of the hazardous state of affairs in their front.[34]

As for the tanks that were to accompany the division, bad luck struck almost immediately. One hundred yards from the jump-off line lay an old minefield of 60-pound plum-pudding bombs, some strung on wire and some partially buried, into which a number of the unsuspecting tanks drove directly. That the mines had been laid previously by the British Fifth Army made such a calamity all the more galling. The American operations report stated that seventeen of the twenty tanks allotted were left immobile as a result. Ten wrecked tanks lay side by side in one section with the bottoms of several torn asunder. Only two tanks got forward with the infantry in this sector.[35] They were of limited use to the infantry as they lost direction and moved obliquely across the front towards the right.[36]

Arguably this excessive loss of tanks should never have happened after the loss of five machines in the prezero sortie by the 4th Tank Battalion.[37] The whereabouts of the minefield ought to have been known. The thick fog was undoubtedly a mitigating factor. However the minefield had been wired and signed by the Germans.[38] It had certainly caused no apparent problems on 27 September when a light fog had prevailed. Lying close to the Blue road it was something the engineers and field companies would have cleared when the ground was won. Unfortunately the minefield lay in contested ground forward of the American jump-off line. Realistically there was little opportunity to work on clearing the zone until the afternoon of 29 September. By then though the damage had been well and truly done.

As had occurred in the preliminary operation, conflicting reports were being received at divisional headquarters as to the degree of success and actual position of the division. Against reports that the Hindenburg Line had been

72

Lieutenant–General Sir John Monash, Commander of the Australian Corps from 31 May 1918 until after the Armistice.

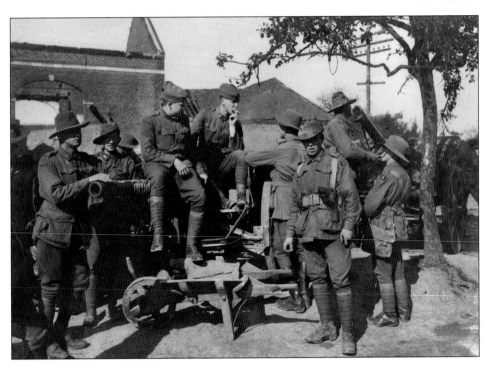

Above: *Americans and Australians at Tincourt.*

Below: *Allied tanks and infantry troops preparing to go into action at Bellicourt, France, on 29 September 1918.*

Above: *The Knoll, situated near Vendhuille, looking towards Bony, a fortified town in the Hindenburg System.*

Below: *Australian soldiers of the 11 Brigade with tanks moving into battle near Bellicourt.*

Above: The northern entrance to the St Quentin Canal Tunnel between Bellicourt and Vendhuilles.

Below: Americans and Australians with German prisoners resting at the southern entrance of the Bellicourt Tunnel.

Above: Soldiers of the 38th Battalion in Dog Trench near Guillemont Farm.

Below: Australian soldiers of the 5th Pioneer Battalion by a fire on the towpath of the St Quentin Canal Tunnel.

Above: A cable section of the 3rd Divisional Signal Company laying a telephone cable near Ronssoy.

Below: The 6 Brigade of Australian Field Artillery bringing up ammunition to the guns through the Hindenburg Line near Bellicourt.

A ditched tank near the main Hindenburg Line.

Above: An armoured car destroyed on a roadside at Bony.

Below: American dead laid out near the road leading to Gillemont Farm and Bony.

reached came news that the left of the 107th Regiment was in retreat. They had lost heavily in officers and were under severe fire from machine guns both on their flank and front. The left of the 27th Division was therefore retiring westwards beyond the line of the Knoll and Gillemont Farm.[39] This retirement began at around 8.50 a.m. – the same time that the Knoll was being claimed as taken.

Air reconnaissance reports shed little light on the confusion. The first air patrol was not able to take off until 8 a.m. due to the impenetrable mist and its reports were not received until mid-morning. Due to low cloud these were largely inconclusive. They were able to report that many tanks had been knocked out west of Bony and that the village appeared still to be in German control. A message was dropped to some of the tanks congregated around the Quennemont Farm position informing them of this fact.[40] A further report was sent at 10.40 a.m. It stated the position as it was somewhat earlier, and claimed that Macquincourt Trench, which lay midway between the Knoll and Vendhuille, was being held and that troops were in the Hindenburg Line south of Macquincourt Farm. These may have been those observed by Pasefield. The troops in Macquincourt Trench might have been part of Blewitt's group with perhaps remnants of some American companies. The British certainly held the position in the mid-afternoon before having to retire around 2 p.m. when the American left had completely collapsed in the forward area.

Attempts were made by the III Corps to relieve the pressure on the struggling doughboys. A battery of British guns under the command of Major F. J. Rice probed forwards to its allotted advance position. If they could survive in this forward position then the rest of the brigade would follow. Rice set up his guns and blew away a trench of Germans with shrapnel fire to secure a new observation post. Around this time the British 55 Brigade was asked to provide a battalion to strike south from the Knoll down to Grub Lane and clear it of Germans. However fire from the vicinity of the Knoll was so intense that the operation was shelved before it had barely begun.[41]

The fierce nature of the German resistance was ascribed in part to the orders, gleaned from those captured, that they had to hold the outpost line at all costs. The upshot of their stubborn opposition was that at 11 a.m. – the time allotted for when the Australians were to pass through the Americans – the 27th Division with but a few exceptions was still held up on the outpost line. On the right, Quennemont Farm had not been subdued though the 2nd Battalion, 108th Regiment was engaged in attempting to mop up the position. A party of the 3rd Battalion, 108th Regiment, led by lieutenants Samuel A. Brown and Harrison J. Uhl, veered southeastwards in the smoke and passed below the farm. They reached the Hindenburg Line capturing a hundred Germans in the process.[42] Other portions of American units did manage to infiltrate through the German lines beyond Lone Tree Trench and get onto the Hindenburg Line.

The situation of the 27th Division by mid-morning was roughly as follows. Some companies of the 3rd Battalion, 108th Regiment were in the Hindenburg Line south of Bony while the left of the battalion had not passed Gillemont Farm. Willow Trench on the western edge of Gillemont Farm was held by the 3rd Battalion, 107th Regiment with the combined battalion of the 106th Regiment. The 2nd Battalion, 107th Regiment extended the line northwards where it was joined with an intermingled combination of 1st Battalion, 107th Regiment and elements of the 105th Regiment south and west of the Knoll.[43] Beyond their left north of the Knoll was the British 54 Brigade.

It was far from clear to the commanders in the rear at the time as to the real nature of affairs on the 27th Division front and what was known was a long way short of what the Australians expected when they reached the vicinity. The exercise of detailing the problems and faults associated with the conduct of the American 30th Division by Australian Brigadier-General Mackay was also undertaken by Brigadier-General Brand in connection with the 27th Division. Brand recorded in detail the ramifications of that formation's operational rawness. After the battle he provided some corrective notes to

General O'Ryan about how the Americans could improve future performance. Among the twenty-six points outlined, the more salient criticisms were: that the staff officers were too headquarters bound, thus often allowing unreliable information to find its way to brigade and divisional headquarters; too much optimism clouded or blinded judgement; too many officers went forward in the first waves and became unnecessary casualties, thus contributing to a shortage of leaders and loss of unit cohesion; and written communications from the field were poor, with too great a reliance on telephone communication and not enough runners. All these things, according to Brand, militated against providing a clear picture of the attack's progress. Combined with poor rear echelon organisation, they further impeded the ability of the Americans to react promptly.[44]

The other assumption that permeated many accounts was that the Americans had rushed forwards in their eagerness to acquit themselves well. This alleged exuberance might well have been so in a few cases. By and large though the men had met with severe and stubborn opposition, which took a heavy toll on them. The division suffered a total of 4,689 casualties, which was equivalent to the dreadful slaughter that had greeted the Australian divisions on the Somme in 1916.[45]

Another possibility that has been suggested is that the Americans were victims of an ambiguous doctrine from Pershing, who oscillated between planning for trench warfare and ascribing to the virtues of and preference for open warfare. As a consequence fighting commanders entered the line with no clear conceptual understanding of their commander-in-chief's expectations. US Army successes were subsequently won by the costly tactic of smothering German machine guns with American flesh.[46] Certainly this aggressive doctrine was patently evident in the early prescriptions for American training, one of the governing principles being that '[a]ll instructions must contemplate the assumption of a vigorous offensive. This purpose will be emphasised in every phase of training until it becomes a settled habit of thought.'[47]

The desire to engage with the Germans in open warfare was evident in the demeanour of the doughboys according to a British officer who observed the training of the 27th Division. He thought the prospect of the fight rather than the immediate, even if seemingly menial, tasks of preparation was a source of distraction to the Americans, 'The men are anxious for active operations rather than the work of trench warfare and have not realised the necessity for acquiring proficiency with the spade.'[48] Deficiencies were undoubtedly carried into battle.

At the Bellicourt Tunnel sector, while doctrinal factors might have contributed in small part to the American losses, the 27th Division's assault was initially compromised by the earlier failure of the British III Corps and subsequent failure of the American 106th Regiment to carry the German strongpoints located at the Knoll, Gillemont Farm and Quennemont Farm. This proved to be, as the Australian official historian C. E. W. Bean termed it, 'a serious complication'.[49]

CHAPTER SIX

Australian 3rd Division

'Christ! What a mess.' – Sergeant Merritt D. Cutler, USA

There was a grim pageantry to the Australian Corp's march to the line on the morning of 29 September. They had started in the clear but soon became enveloped in the sudden fog that quickly shrouded the battlefield. Mist clung in all the folds of the hills and valleys. Vapours rose from the ground, which had been drenched with gas for two nights by the German guns and which was now again soaked with mustard gas. Over this steaming landscape trudged the Australians. They had breakfasted behind their artillery line and sometime after 7 a.m. set off towards the start line. Leading the khaki mass were the tanks. Grouped together in their respective sections they made for their predetermined rendezvous points. Six brigades of artillery filled the four approach roads, the horse teams straining at the bit under the guidance of cursing drivers. British cavalry was in the mix, too, hoping to strike into the German rear areas to exploit the anticipated gains. The fields were choked with snaking lines of infantrymen in artillery formation, following in the tracks of the tanks, making their way towards their start line which they were not to cross until 9 a.m. Gas and smoke drifting back off the front line forced many of the men to don their gas masks – casting them as minions of a ghastly faceless legion. Behind this other worldly instrument of destruction followed an almost Gatsby-like motorcade of war correspondents, official photographers and distinguished visitor's going forward to observe the panorama of the frontline.[1]

Forming the left wing of the corps was the Australian 3rd Division, General Sir John Monash's old command. It was now commanded by Major-General John Gellibrand. Tasmanian born, schooled in Britain and fluent in German and French, Gellibrand was one of the finest senior commanders to have graced the AIF. If there was anyone who understood the mindset and *modus operandi* of the Australian commander-in-chief it was Gellibrand and the officers and men of his division. To mark it as distinct Monash had initially insisted the men wear the brim of their broad hats down turned rather than looped as was the custom in the other divisions. The division was a model of efficiency and it was its professional organisation and conduct that had helped win Monash the top job. It represented a microcosm of the Australian Corps he came to sculpt.

The first intimation that the 3rd Division received of trouble ahead – they still being two miles short of their intended jump-off line – was when its lead battalions passed Ronssoy and commenced the descent into the valley behind the American left flank. Crouching alongside the roadside in whatever cover was available were the engineers waiting for the way ahead to be cleared so they might get on with their work repairing the Blue road. These units were responsible for maintaining and repairing the roads for the guns and vehicular traffic that was to push forward in close support of the expected breakthrough. Their spirits were lifted by the sight of the 'old hands' passing by to restore order to the apparent snag up ahead.[2]

The Australian infantry moved down the Gillemont road, passing through the 18-pounder batteries situated there, and on towards Z Copse. As they moved forwards, gas and high-explosive shells began bursting among them. Veteran ears soon discerned the telltale rattle of machine guns ahead, 'I can hear too many Boche machine guns,' commented one officer pessimistically.[3]

The division quickly shook itself into battle mode. The 9 Brigade, commanded by Brigadier-General Henry Arthur Goddard, was situated the furthest north and was acting as the divisional reserve. Tall and lean with a face marked by a thick dark moustache, Goddard had been prominent in saving Amiens during the German spring offensive.[4] His brigade's approach march was from the northwest beyond Lempire. Once the leading brigades – the 10 Brigade on the left and the 11 Brigade on the right – passed the old outpost line, the 9 Brigade was to fall in behind and then guard the northern flank as the main attack pushed east. Goddard described the Americans he saw as 'lost sheep, not knowing where to go or what to do'.[5] Many Australians made similar comments but it should be remembered that the rear of any fighting unit, especially one that has lost heavily, was the most likely place to witness shaken morale in an exaggerated state.

The units in the 10 and 11 Brigades were the first to come under fire from the German artillery. The brigade signallers too pulled up short unable to get forward to set up the communication centre – just as the engineer and pioneer units had earlier been brought to a standstill by the barrage.[6] At 9 a.m. the Australians reached the American start line as per the battle schedule. Here they saw clearly that all was not well. South of the Gillemont road near Duncan Post lay the disabled tanks that had earlier been caught in the minefield. Groups of Americans were streaming back from the front. Many fell to enemy fire as the Australians watched. Information from the returning doughboys was sketchy and few could give any concise details as to what had occurred. What was certain to the Australians was that a major reverse had befallen the 27th Division.

One among the returning throng was Captain Leland of the American 107th Regiment. He met an advance patrol of the 40th Battalion and was directed back to its headquarters. This was set up in a large crater next to an aid post on the sheltered side of the slope down which the Australians must advance and over which the Americans had passed before them. Captain J. S. Reed, the 40th Battalion's regimental surgeon, was working feverishly on the large numbers of American wounded that his stretcher bearers were collecting as well as those brought in, forlorn and bleeding, by their mates.[7]

79

Leland's enquiry as to the whereabouts of his regiment was met curtly by Lieutenant-Colonel J. E. C. Lord. The Australian colonel was in an unpleasant frame of mind and, according to Leland, damning all and everything around him.

'Your troops have been repulsed,' snapped Lord. 'We are going to prepare right here for the counterattack, which is probably on the way now. One of your officers is collecting all the Americans he can find. I want you to man and hold this line of trenches here on the left.'

At that moment a badly wounded Australian officer reported in. His head was swathed in bandages, his arm in a sling and blood and gore were spattered over his uniform. Barely able to stand, he was supported by one of his men. Sympathy was in short supply.

'What the ___ do you mean by getting yourself shot up again?' raged Lord. 'Haven't I repeatedly told you to stop exposing yourself? You have been in this game long enough to know better. Who the devil do you think is going to take your company now?'[8]

It is unclear who this hapless officer was. The most likely candidate is Captain Clarkborough who was later referred to in a field telephone communique as being badly wounded in the neck. Another valuable officer lost was 2nd Lieutenant H. Boden of D Company. It was his platoon that Leland may have passed on his way to the 40th Battalion's HQ. Boden was mortally wounded by machine-gun fire while personally bombing the Germans back from the junction of Grub Lane and Willow Trench. Twice wounded at Gallipoli and thrice in France, Boden's luck had finally run out.[9]

Leland reconnected with the fragments of Americans in the trenches north of Gillemont road. Here the sorry tale of many of his comrades became known to him. Meanwhile the Australians were busily engaged in getting a defensive line in order. They had been prevailed on to keep their formations from becoming entangled with the Americans as they passed through. Under the present circumstances though this proved exceedingly difficult.

A sense of the chaotic nature of things was captured in a description by Sergeant Merritt D. Cutler, 107th Regiment, 'The Australians had mingled in with the Germans in the rear. Everyone was shooting at someone. To make it worse, the shell holes were loaded with wounded men . . . Christ, what a mess!'

The Australian line was not mingled with the German. That claim being a good example of the exaggeration that could creep into postwar accounts, but the wounded were many and the situation was an undoubted mess. Although wounded Cutler tried valiantly to assist others to safety. Desperate for help he called on two incoming Australians, one of whom did not want any part of going into 'that mess'. The other however was more helpful and replied, 'Sure Yank, I'll go; we're in this bloody thing together.'[10]

The 40th Battalion formed the left of the Australian and 10 Brigade line. It was deployed north of the Gillemont road. Captain H. L. Foster's A Company anchored its right on the road and took cover in Dog Trench, which ran northeasterly from the road about three hundred yards due west of the farm, and Willow Trench. Extending left from his company was Captain Findlay's C Company, then Captain McIntyre's B Company with Captain Ruddock's D Company the far left. Smoke drifting back from the front obscured their view of the field south of Gillemont Farm. However in their immediate front the counterattack Lord had feared was on its way could be seen developing down Macquincourt valley.

Ruddock's D Company was dispatched to Willow Trench to meet this advance. As part of the same movement Findlay's C Company swung behind Ruddock and shifted to the left of the line with its front facing to the Knoll. The scene in Willow Trench was a chaotic and bloody one. It was crammed with disoriented men both wounded and unwounded. Dead lay all around and the numbers in the trench increased as more and more Americans found its sanctuary as they ran or crawled back from the front and dropped down on those already huddled there. Ever conscious of getting their defensive line in order the Australians began to direct any American wounded capable of walking out of the trench. The incapacitated Americans were told to crawl back to the dead ground in the valley about two hundred yards in rear. Meanwhile the surviving doughboys, bucked by the Australians arrival, began to rally. Australian and American machine guns were placed on the parapet to form a formidable defensive line.

The Germans were now pushing numbers across Macquincourt valley towards the Knoll. They already held Lone Tree Trench and were bombing their way forwards down Grub Lane towards Willow Trench. It was here that Lieutenant Boden had come to grief. His good work was taken up by Corporal A. J. Barwick and a party of bombers. They succeeded in securing a sixty-yard stretch of Grub Lane and blocked it off setting up a forward post there. Further to the left another German forward thrust was thwarted when Private P. Dransfield with others engaged them with the bayonet.[11]

Beyond Willow Trench, Lieutenant Frank Lakin had brought up a platoon of C Company to extend the left. He watched the Americans breaking back from the Knoll support trench from which they were driven. He was dismayed to see some Americans greeting the German attack by standing up and firing their rifles, thus completely exposing themselves to the scything machine-gun fire. Lakin's men formed posts in shell holes across the slope facing Knoll Trench. In these were collected about two hundred American stragglers who were used to fortify the position further. This amalgam of Aussies and Yanks along with the fire from Ruddock's company in Willow Trench was able to halt the German advance up Macquincourt valley for the time being.[12] At 1 p.m., north of the Knoll, the 7th Queens attempted to extend the British line south to link with the Americans and Australians. The fire coming off the Knoll and behind was simply too hot and they were forced to ground for the rest of the afternoon.[13]

To the right of the 40th Battalion, the 39th Battalion had moved up. They, too, were under heavy fire as they advanced from the Duncan Post vicinity. Led by Lieutenant-Colonel R. O. Henderson, they moved into Dog Trench which ran southwesterly in front of Gillemont Farm. They straddled the Gillemont road about three hundred yards west of the farm. Here they set about consolidating a defensive position while trying to establish a clear picture of what lay ahead of them. From the retiring Americans and the snatches of information being received at brigade HQ they were of the belief that some Americans lay ahead. Exactly where and how many remained a mystery as the heavy fire in front suggested a solid and unbroken enemy front. Patrols were pushed forwards to try to ascertain the whereabouts of any Americans and to report on the strength of the Germans. Henderson, who had set up his command post in a shell hole, was killed – shot through the head – by a German sniper while trying to observe the enemy line. Command of the battalion temporarily fell to Captain C. L. Giles. The returning patrols brought back news that the Germans manned the first line of trenches in front of Gillemont Farm and that they were also present in strength down the length of the sunken road to Bony, all their positions being studded with machine guns.[14]

The 38th Battalion lay on the right of the 39th in Dog Trench south of the Gillemont road. As the trench ran southwesterly and away from the German's main outpost line position they were necessarily further from the enemy than those units on their left. They looked out on the depressing sight of the tanks disabled and burning in the old minefield. Its lead company, A Company led by Captain Fairweather, advanced from shell hole to shell hole by half sectional rushes. They managed to get their line to within fifty yards of South Gillemont Trench, which ran down from the farm. In doing so they lost their commanding officer and another, Lieutenant Callan, as well as several men. Behind them C Company was crouched low in Dog Trench under a heavy shell fire.

Opposite the Quennemont Farm position a similar story of hard fighting was unfolding on the 11 Brigade front. Commanding this brigade was Brigadier-General J. H. Cannan. Advancing on a two-battalion front, the 41st Battalion on the left and the 44th Battalion on the right, the brigade was forced to ground by the machine-gun and artillery barrage brought down by the Germans. In the face of the murderous fire on their front, every effort was made to get the line forwards. Lieutenant M. J. Flannery led a platoon of the 41st into Quennet Copse and began to work down the trench there but was stopped by thick wire and determined bombing resistance from the enemy. Another officer, Lieutenant Dodds, stood on the parapet of the trench to urge the men forwards but fell to a sniper's bullet as did one of the Lewis gunners who had clambered from the trench firing from the hip at the enemy machine guns. The 41st Battalion managed to advance its line about two hundred yards but could go no further.[15]

Meanwhile the 44th Battalion pushed on to Quennemont Farm. It was meant to pass south of the farm and was swept with machine-gun fire from that position as it arrived. All around lay the American dead from the earlier advance. The battalion's two left companies sank into shell holes in front of the farm while its two right companies diverged southeast in the fog. Led by Captain Lewis and Lieutenant W. J. Hunt these diggers encountered little resistance and passed through the outpost line and then the Hindenburg Line to the tunnel mound. They had found the point of entry where the Americans had punched through in the initial attack.[16]

Back at Quennemont Farm the two left companies of the 44th Battalion were joined by Lieutenant-Colonel Scanlan of the 59th Battalion. Scanlan's battalion was the reserve for the 15 Brigade in the adjacent sector of the 5th Division. He had been looking for a tank to assist his men forwards and, finding one, directed it to the sound of the machine guns audible to his left at the farm. He was lucky to survive. A warning shout from one of his men caused him to drop into the wire tearing his trousers and cutting his hands. A German rifleman had been spotted taking aim at him. Lewis gunners dealt quickly with the threat and the colonel moved on.[17]

Acting similarly, Lieutenant Buckingham marched his company of the 59th Battalion to the sound of the guns. Together Buckingham's company and the

44th Battalion, with the assistance of two tanks forwarded to the area by Major F. E. Hotblack, a staff officer of Tank Corps HQ, captured forty Germans and began to mop up the farm area.[18] The surviving Germans of the 7th and 60th Regiments gradually fell back northeastwards towards Bony.[19] The collapse of the German stronghold at Quennemont Farm now exposed the left of the German defenders holding the southern portion of South Gillemont Trench opposite Quennet Copse, where the Australians had a toehold. Under cover of the fog the 41st Battalion had been able to move off, directly east, undetected into the Hindenburg Line second trenches.

The veil of mist that had clothed the battlefield for the better part of the morning began to evaporate. The 11 Brigade men in the main German line and those that had made it onto the tunnel mound were now under direct observation. German batteries in Cabaret Wood fired over open sights at them and to the north other batteries and machine guns directed their fire at these groups. The Australians had picked up some elements of the American 108th Regiment when they got through the line and now this combined force prepared to defend its gains. Northwest of them they could see lines of German carrying parties moving up to supply the forward areas where the rest of the 3rd Division was hung up. The Australians turned their guns onto these groups in a long-distance attempt to disrupt the supply.

Looking back from whence he had come, Sergeant J. E. V. K. (Yak) Ingvarsen could see that a German machine gun was holding up the advance of some Australians and Americans trying to join those already forward. The bulk of these were probably the rest of the 44th and 59th Battalions picking their way forwards after capturing Quennemont Farm joined by groups of doughboys who had broken through earlier in the morning. Ingvarsen sprinted back 100 yards over open ground and bombed the machine gunner. The rest of the Germans at the post tried to withdraw up the trench but were confronted by Ingvarsen running along the parapet 'snapshooting' at them as he ran. His action cleared 150 yards of the Hindenburg Line trenches and paved the way for the advance.[20]

One sight the Allies wished they were spared was of a group of armoured cars and whippet tanks from the 5 Tank Brigade that drove purposely towards Bony. The village was being held by portions of both the 27th and 60th German Regiments. The 27th Regiment history described the armoured advance as one made 'ignorant of the position'.[21] The tanks involved belonged to B Company of the 3rd Tank Battalion under Major C. H. May. They were to have rendezvoused with the armoured cars at 9.15 a.m. The armoured cars (17th Battalion) had moved off without communicating with the tanks. On discovering that the cars had moved off towards Bony, the tanks were ordered to follow. Unsupported and plainly visible once they breasted the crest the approaching vehicles were picked off in rapid succession by the German gunners. Four cars and four of the tanks were destroyed with the remainder beating a hasty retreat back to the area around Quennemont Farm.[22]

With the Germans in control of the village it was not long before a determined bombing attack was launched down the two main trenches of the Hindenburg Line against the Australian breaches. This was carried out by the 1st and 2nd Battalions of the 87th Regiment which had been brought up from reserve to support the 60th Regiment south of Bony.[23] Their attack fell on the left sections of the 44th Battalion and forced it back fifty yards. As fighting intensified two more companies belonging to 3rd Battalion, 87th Regiment were summoned from Le Catelet–Nauroy Line north of Cabaret Wood. Two German company commanders were killed in the fighting.[24] From the Australian perspective the situation was stabilised and the ground reclaimed through a counterattack by the 59th Battalion. Lieutenant Parr's company with support from Captain Robert's company and a platoon led by Lieutenant Chambers were prominent in this effort.[25] By 2 p.m. the Germans had refused their flank to face southwards towards the Australians. A company of 3rd Battalion, 87th Regiment held a communication trench connecting the two main trenches of

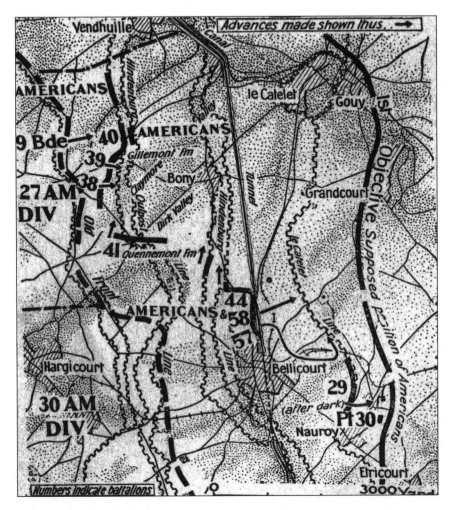

MAP 7 *Position of Australian battalions early afternoon, 29 September*

the Hindenburg Line with another two companies drawn along the open spur east of that supported by a company of the 241st Engineers.[26]

The combined force of the 44th and 59th Battalions had pushed on to join the rest of the 44th in the Hindenburg Line. For a short while the 44th Battalion was able to use the communication trench of Top Lane to screen its advance. However when the 41st Battalion with two machine guns from the 9th Machine Gun Company had attempted to force their way up Top Lane, which connected the outpost line with the main German defence system, they were unable to counter the anti-tank and machine-gun fort that dominated the approach.[27] Captain C. Longmore, author of the 44th Battalion history and company commander at the time, believed the Germans had fought with 'more dash and vim [here] . . . than he'd ever produced before'.[28] The 41st Battalion's inability to push past this point meant that, effectively, the Germans held the intervening ground between the 41st and 44th Battalions. These seemingly small Australian gains were nevertheless ultimately significant as they provided a hinge on which the neighbouring 5th Division could pivot.

As perplexing as the situation was during the morning for the troops in the field it was equally vexing for the headquarter staffs trying to unravel the conflicting reports filtering through to them. Monash, whose rising stress was visible before the attack had even commenced, now found his normally considered – even if often abrupt – responses in danger of giving way to a fulminating rage. A British officer privy to Monash's response to the American setback at the time recalled:

> At Divisional HQ I heard the candid opinion of Sir John Monash . . . on their [the Americans'] prowess. It was not the polite though thinly veiled opinion which appeared in the *Sunday Times* at 28 December 1919. Never have I heard such an elegant flow of language, either in the army, or out of it. He called them all the names under the sun . . . nothing was too bad for them.[29]

Monash was obviously exasperated when he issued this diatribe. Conflicting reports as to the exact nature of affairs on the American front clearly suggested that the second phase of the operation had been undermined. While there was undoubtedly confusion on the ground among the troops it was also evident that the greenness of the Americans had revealed a significant weakness in their grasp of battlefield logistics which made the planning of an adequate response to the changed circumstances a problematic exercise.

The disappointment expressed at the failure communicated through these reports was possibly all the greater for the unexpected success of the 46th Division earlier in the morning, which had been quickly communicated to the various command HQs. The elation of cracking what was considered the hardest nut in the German defence had doubtless raised expectations for corresponding success in the adjacent sectors. Reports that the 30th Division had made the Green Line were understandably accepted as likely given the 46th Division's victorious attack. There seemed little evidence at hand to doubt the veracity of the statements filtering through. Clearly though the Australian 3rd Division was confronted by heavy opposition. This extended across its own front and down into the sector of the 5th Division, which was following in behind the American 30th Division. Monash's chief of staff, Major-General Blamey, was busily trying to make sense of the reports being sent back by the 3rd Division commanders. It was perhaps in these exchanges that the first great misrepresentation of the Americans as having failed to mop up began to be aired.

The intelligence that most shaped the misunderstanding of what was happening was that brought back by the pilots around mid-morning. This information placed American troops in Guoy. That coupled with the supposed success of the 30th Division created an initial belief that the Green Line had been reached in some strength. If the Green Line had been attained then it was assumed that the resistance being met by the Australians was simply isolated pockets that the Americans had failed to mop up. However to mop up one must necessarily have been in control of the ground in question and of this the Americans had never been.

The reality was that the 27th Division had been repulsed all along its front but for a few groups that had pierced the line and plunged headlong into the Germans around Guoy or those moving westwards as they reinforced the line.

Furthermore the Germans were mounting a counterattack up the valleys to attempt to drive their attackers back further. The fact that they had survived this attempt with their line largely in tact meant they were also able to enfilade the flank of the American 30th Division further south and also the incoming Australian 5th Division, which was following behind.

CHAPTER SEVEN

Australian 5th Division

'Shoot me, please.' – British tank officer

Major-General Talbot Hobbs brought the Australian 5th Division forwards through the artillery lines intending to jump off the Green Line, which the American 30th Division was expected to have reached by 9 a.m. Instead the Australians found themselves under fire soon after passing the outpost line. In this, their experience mirrored that of their countrymen in the neighbouring sector. One salient difference was that due to the American 30th Division having started on the outpost line the 5th Division was further forward than their compatriots.

Only four weeks had passed since the 5th Division won perhaps the finest victory of the Australian Army's short and illustrious history. Against all odds, undermanned and exhausted it had stormed the German fortress at Mont St Quentin and Peronne, breaking the vital Somme line and opening the way for further advances. Its battalions had been founded from a nucleus of Anzac veterans and topped up with new recruits. Its introduction to the Western Front in 1916 had been harsh. At Fromelles a combination of dull-witted British generalship coupled with the inexperience of its own commanders and men saw the division come, in the parlance of the day, a real gutzer. Insultingly written off as 'an important raid' in a general communiqué the battle cost 5,533 Australian casualties in a single, bloody night. Its commander at the time was General James W. McCay. In December 1916 he was forced to relinquish his command due to ill-health and return to Australia. Command of the division passed to Talbot Hobbs.

Hobbs was an architect, an English immigrant and resident of Perth, Western Australia. He had previously commanded the artillery at Gallipoli and the 1st Division's guns at Pozieres and Mouquet Farm. Hobbs had returned to his division on the eve of the Bellicourt Tunnel battle having been away on leave for a short time. He and his brigadiers were no strangers to hard fighting. The redoubtable Pompey Elliot's 15 Brigade took up the left of the division with the 59th and 57th Battalions in the lead. Next was Brigadier-General Tivey's 8 Brigade with two battalions out front and two in support. Brigadier-General Stewart's 14 Brigade formed the division reserve.

The lead elements of the 5th Division first came under fire as they breasted the crest of Sentinel Ridge 1,000 yards west of Bellicourt. Of particular concern was the fact that the enemy fire was coming from three unexpected directions. On the left the Germans in Bony and surrounds were proving a major source of embarrassment. In front, on the slopes before Nauroy where the Americans were meant to be, a steady fire spewed forth while in and around Bellicourt heavy machine-gun fire continued unabated. As well German artillery was finding its mark which meant observers were still operating with immunity. Adding to the burden of the incoming troops was the congestion on the Bellicourt road. The roadside was choked with stretcher cases and their bearers and the road with walking wounded and stragglers. It took three hours to clear this clutter of human misery and restore the route to a reasonably orderly state.[1]

As we have seen the morning progress of the 15 Brigade's 59th Battalion belonged to the story of the Australian 3rd Division. On its right however was the 57th Battalion. Because the 59th Battalion had slewed northeastwards, the 58th Battalion was pushed into the gap. The 58th Battalion had come under fire in front of Malakoff Farm, which was an advanced position half a mile southwest of Quennemet Farm and a little north of a mile west of Bellicourt.

As the Quennemont Farm position was suppressed by the troops on the left, the fire slackened and the 58th Battalion was able to get up to the Hindenburg Line at the spot known as Mount Olympus. Here it linked with the 44th Battalion and elements of the 59th Battalion which had banded together and pushed east from Quennemont Farm. On its right was the 57th Battalion, which had earlier skirted north of Bellicourt and reached the tunnel mound position. Several hundred Americans, most belonging to the American 119th Regiment, were crouched along the bank of the tunnel peering anxiously eastwards. They reported that other Americans lay ahead of them. Indeed a group of doughboys was lying about three hundred yards ahead trapped against the railway embankment and pinned down by German machine guns firing from Le Catelet–Nauroy Line 200 yards beyond them.[2] These were the vanguard of the American 120th Regiment. This then was the extent of the American advance in the American 30th Division's northern sector. It hardly justified claims that the Green Line had been gained. There was little that the 57th and 58th Battalion could do but sit tight.

Lieutenant-Colonel Denehy had cleverly guided the 57th Battalion through the fog by following a line of telegraph poles that had been observed in an earlier reconnaissance. Although he could not see from one pole to the next he was able to keep direction by following the broken wire that lay tangled on the ground. If his men had to sit and endure an uncertain future he intended to make them as comfortable as possible. He found a box of cigars in a trench and as his men came up dispensed one to each soldier. Soon the Australians were puffing away and, while in this moment of repose, three Germans stumbled out of the fog into their midst. With a polite '*Pardon messieurs*' the surprised trio raised their hands thankful to accept their fate and be directed to the rear.[3]

South of Bellicourt the situation was also confused. Here the success of the 46th Division had temporarily unhinged the left of the German line opposite the American 30th Division. Consequently the American 120th Regiment had got forward only to come up short opposite Nauroy. Behind them the American 117th Regiment became embroiled in a fight to clear Bellicourt as German defenders and reinforcements stood steadfastly by their guns. A section of this regiment had however taken the tunnel entrance and peeled southwards to link with the British 46th Division's left.

Given the fierce resistance being put up in the American 27th Division and Australian 3rd Division sector and given the considerable opposition in front of Nauroy and in Bellicourt, there was little scope for concerted action by the left battalions of the 5th Division. For the moment they hunkered down as best they could along the tunnel mound with the remnants of the American units. It was on the right where the success of the 46th Division had exposed the German left that the greatest opportunity for exploitation existed.

As the Australian 8 Brigade marched up by Quarry Wood, 1,000 yards west of Bellicourt, it was apparent that all had not gone well ahead of them. Disorganised and leaderless groups of Americans were retiring, having lost touch with their units. They, according to the arriving diggers, did not know what to do. The southern end of Bellicourt was clearly in Allied possession and the streets were crowded with wagons, guns and tanks trying to get to their prearranged destinations. Here the 8 Brigade's lead unit, the 29th Battalion, rendezvoused with its four whippet tanks. However sections within the village still contained many Germans as did the trenches immediately north and west of the town.[4]

Disaster soon visited the tanks as they emerged from the village. The mist cleared and the machines fell under the direct sight of the gunners of the German 55th Battery in a tank fort strategically placed at the edge of Nauroy Wood north of that village. The Germans placed this attack at 11 a.m.[5] Within minutes two tanks were destroyed. Seeing the hopelessness of the situation an infantry officer of the 29th Battalion hurried up to one of the tanks and urged the officer commanding not to go on but to wait until the infantry had dealt with the fort. 'I must go on, if I think there is a chance and, you know,

94

there is a chance', replied the tank commander. The tank advanced a further thirty yards before it was struck by a direct hit. With a flash and roar the petrol within ignited engulfing the crew inside. The door opened and out staggered the officer, wounded, blinded and ablaze from head to toe. He collapsed in front of the horrified infantrymen. 'Shoot me, please', pleaded the stricken officer. One of the men obliged.[6]

A fourth tank commanded by Captain Grenfell, who had been wounded, managed to reach the safety of some dead ground 100 yards beyond the village and remained with the battalion for the rest of the day. A section of guns belonging to the 49th Battery of the Australian 13 Artillery Brigade had also trotted forwards with the tanks. They had inadvertently passed the infantry in the fog and suddenly found themselves amidst a torrent of bursting shells. Man and beast turned hurriedly to find safety. Further down the road leading into Bellicourt the rest of the Australian guns were scattered by direct fire. After a hurried conversation between Colonel Caddy, the Australian 13 Field Artillery Brigade commander, and the acting commander of the 29th Battalion, Captain Charles Derham, it was thought best to retire the guns behind the Hindenburg outpost line until the situation improved.[7]

Unlike the American commanders, the Germans had no compunction about shelling an area in which their own troops might have been (and indeed were). The scene in Bellicourt has been eloquently described in the history of the 30th Battalion. That unit, then approaching from the southwest in support of the 29th Battalion, witnessed the following sight:

> Slightly to our north the one-time peaceful village of Bellicourt loomed up on the tortured landscape – a mass of flame. This rural hamlet, surrounded by stately trees and gardens of content, held the dubious honour of being a prominent landmark on a modern battlefield. Periodically it received weighty attention from the tireless German gunners. We watched detached buildings bulge and sway in an agony of movement and miraculously retain the crazy

95

perpendicular of a tipsy reveller; others suddenly mushroomed, to collapse like a pricked tyre. Faint silhouettes scampered about like rabbits on the fringe of the village.[8]

Faced with this mayhem around his approach march, Derham ordered patrols forward to ascertain what lay ahead of the 29th Battalion. These quickly confirmed his worst suspicions that the Green Line had not been reached and that Nauroy was clearly in enemy hands. Undeterred he set about pushing his line forwards. Indicative of just how confused the situation had become was the fact that a German machine-gun crew from the 251st Regiment began setting up only thirty yards' distance from Derham's Battalion HQ. The audacious crew was spotted by some returning runners and quickly captured.[9]

The 29th Battalion split into two groups. One moved cautiously eastwards towards Nauroy, down a communication trench and track that paralleled it. Crowded along the length of the trench and track were about 250 Americans. The track ran directly into a juncture of Le Catelet and Nauroy system and on to the tank fort in the corner of Nauroy Wood. The fort, which had suffered heavily in previous fighting judging by the numerous dead lying in the surrounding trenches, was captured after a brief and bitter close action. In it were two 77-mm field guns belonging to the 55th Field Artillery Regiment, two trench mortars and numerous anti-tank rifles and machine guns. Thirteen prisoners were captured. Having cleared this obstacle the Australians worked their way northwards until halted about a thousand yards short of Cabaret Wood by the artillery and machine guns posted there.[10]

The second group of the 29th Battalion diverged southeastwards down the sunken road that led to Nauroy. They reached the juncture of the road and Le Catelet–Nauroy Line. Here they found a defensive post that had been set up earlier by two fighting patrols of the 30th Battalion. Led by lieutenants J. C. Yeomans and A. H. Forbes these patrols had struck out after their battalion HQ had received a message from Major Wark's 32nd Battalion stating that his left flank was in the air. The patrols arrived after the 32nd Battalion had passed south of the village and managed to cut off some Germans in the trenches, capturing eighteen of the enemy.

With the arrival of two tanks, Yeomans decided to attack the village. The Australian lieutenant hopped on top of one tank and directed it over the trenches and into the town. He personally rushed one machine-gun post and soon cleared the area after leading his men through the streets and trenches. The village was captured by 12.45 p.m. Posts were set up northeast of the town and these were handed over to the 29th Battalion men. By mid-afternoon with their left in the air – the 15 Brigade battalions being held up along the tunnel line behind them – and with their right still not in touch with the 32nd Battalion, Derham halted his troops.[11]

Between Bellicourt and the southern tunnel entrant a special smoke screen had been laid by the Royal Engineers to mask the operation against the tunnel entrant. This, coupled with the fog, produced an even thicker shroud of invisibility than in other parts of the battlefield. Into this plunged Major Wark and the 32nd Battalion over which he held temporary command. The battalion had to fight its way past Bellicourt, which it did with the aid of a tank that was pressed into service when it was heard passing in the fog. West of the tunnel line about two hundred leaderless men of the American 117th Regiment were collected and attached to the battalion. Again in the fog the sound of tank engines was heard. The section of tanks allotted to the American 117th Regiment, which had missed the 'hop over', was now lumbering forwards. It was 10 a.m. and the tanks were placed in advance of the infantry. Together they cleared a number of enemy machine-gun posts between the village and the tunnel entrant. Half an hour later Wark's men met up with their own tanks. These were now only two in number. With the tanks out front, the 32nd Battalion advanced south of Nauroy on a two-company front with two companies in successive lines in reserve. The Americans were able to join the rest of their regiment, which was found on the canal line where it had earlier captured the tunnel entrant – one of the few clear successes on the American programme.[12]

The leading tank was put out of action as it worked along the ridge south of Nauroy towards the Estrees road. Wark responded immediately, sending Captain A. T. Rogers with the reserve companies and the other tank into the southern outskirts of the town. Rogers paid with his life but the opposition was quashed and forty prisoners taken. This represented the second attack on the village, which the Germans placed as occurring at 11.45 a.m.[13] The 32nd Battalion continued southeastwards. Because of the 46th Division success little opposition was encountered in this area, the bulk of the Germans having retired further eastwards. Wark continued on while the going was good and passed by Hilliard Copse until he linked with the left of the 4th Leicester Regiment of the British 137 Brigade.

Behind the Leicesters the ground was teeming with tanks, artillery, support troops and reserves indicative of a major victory. Watching the avalanche of khaki moving forward, Wark was buoyed by the likelihood that his battalion at least would make its objectives for the day. With the British protecting his right he and his men turned eastwards. A German 77-mm four-gun battery firing from Etricourt was causing heavy casualties to his rear companies and so with some of his men Wark rushed up the slopes and overwhelmed the guns, capturing ten of the crew while scattering and killing the rest. From here Wark took two NCOs and dashed south across the valley towards the village of Magny la Fosse, where he captured a further fifty startled Germans, probably belonging to the 33rd Fusilier Regiment and the 44th Regiment. Not wishing to lose the initiative he quickly called up one company and pushed it through the village to the ridge east of the town.[14]

One observer of Wark's attack was Major Charrington of the 5 Cavalry Brigade. He had gone forwards as part of a liaison group of two officers and five men. They were to advise their brigade of the chances of exploitation and of possible routes should the moment arrive to push the cavalry through. Of

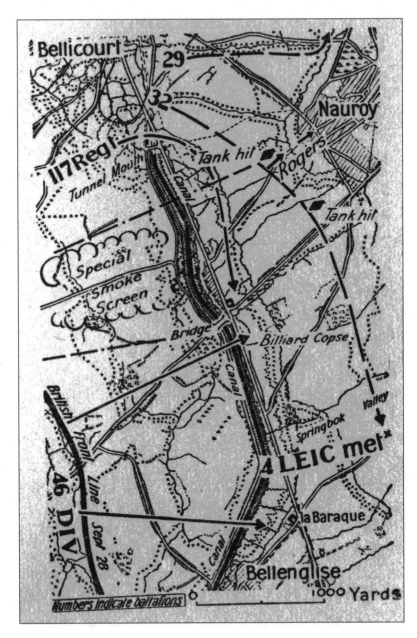

MAP 8 *The Australian 32nd Battalion's attack linking with 46th Division*

that group all but Charrington became casualties during the course of the day. After the war he submitted a glowing account of the attack to the Australian 8 Brigade commander:

> The Australians . . . began moving down the long bare slope towards Nauroy in column of route, intending to form up behind the ridge there and deploy for their attack on the second objective. At this moment the mist lifted, to disclose the Germans in full strength up the Nauroy Ridge and the Australian columns were at once subjected to very heavy rifle and machine-gun fire. Had they attempted to retire, the effort must have been disastrous, although such an action would have seemed the most obvious course to most troops under the circumstance. Instead of this they deployed straightaway for an attack, went direct for Nauroy Ridge, and thanks to the rapidity both of the commander's decision with which all orders were issued and carried out and to the skilful use made of the ground, the ridge was captured and all intervening ground properly mopped up in an incredibly short space of time, and with surprisingly little loss. It was one of the most brilliant performances it was my good fortune ever to see.[15]

Thereafter patrols were sent towards Joncourt, which was found to be firmly in German control. With his left in the air, Wark had regularly sent runners back to inform the reserve battalions of the 32nd Battalion's situation. On his right the British 32nd Division was leapfrogging through the 46th Division on to the army's objective for the day. Its left brigade advanced the line a further mile eastwards with the aid of some whippet tanks, while the other – led by the 15th Highland Light Infantry Battalion – stormed Le Tronquoy Ridge, which overlooked a one-mile underground section of the canal.[16]

A brief attempt was made by the cavalry to join the advance but their presence and contribution were the subject of some cynicism:

About 4,000 cavalry were pouring along the road . . . two abreast, they were an abominable nuisance, as they slowed down all the traffic . . . the General in command of the cavalry, after he had lost about eight men, reported that he could not break through, and he and his men, after having been infernally in the way for a day or so, once more proceeded to obstruct the roads in departing. I do not know if this decision was justified, but I think the officer who commanded the Fort Garry horse would have managed to do something more than this. What would it have mattered if the whole lot including their General had been wiped out provided a breakthrough could have been affected.[17]

The cavalry was the British 5 Cavalry Brigade commanded by Brigadier-General Neil Haig, cousin of the British commander-in-chief, and they were working in conjunction with the Australian 8 Infantry Brigade. Monash had assigned the responsibility of determining whether the cavalry could be used for exploitation to the 8 Brigade commander. Given the circumstances on his front Tivey could only conclude that this was not the occasion for the use of the horsemen and it was he who did not let them go.[18]

The advance by Wark's intrepid band, made under the gaze of the cavalrymen, marked the furthest any of the Australian battalions reached on 29 September. With the 29th Battalion pushing north and the 32nd Battalion's thrust south, a yawning gap had opened between the left and right of the 15 Brigade's front. Into this gap was sent D Company of the 30th Battalion but their story belongs to the next phase.

CHAPTER EIGHT

Diggers and Doughboys

'It is absolute suicide.' – Brigadier-General McNicoll

Throughout the morning until mid-afternoon of 29 September, Monash's corps HQ clung to the belief that the Green Line was held by the Americans and, despite what seemed obvious contradictory information from its own local commanders, that the opposition faced must only be pockets of Germans that had not been mopped up.

On the left flank news from the 10 Brigade was emphatic about the strength of the Germans facing them. General McNicoll spoke directly to the 3rd Division general staff officer (grade 1) (GSO1), Lieutenant-Colonel Jess, and stated:

> The whole eight tanks allotted to me have been knocked out – most of the crews burnt before they got near Gillemont Farm and Willow Trench. I have sent orders to feel forward by patrols. Captain Clarkborough is badly wounded in the neck and his company was not able to advance more than 100 yards owing to heavy m.g. fire. I have no arty to use and cannot use it until we know what the situation is. Can I get hold of the tanks of the 9 Brigade?[1]

The 9 Brigade tanks would not be forthcoming as that formation, unable to push through the breach as initially planned owing to the resistance in the Knoll and Vendhuille sectors, was earmarked to move across the 3rd Division rear to ready itself for an attack northwards from the juncture of the 3rd and 5th Division fronts – Jess having anticipated the likely response from his corps commander. The Australians were also without adequate artillery support because the division's guns were stacked up behind the ridge unable to get forwards because of the German dominance over that part of the field.

The precarious situation on the American front was again communicated by General McNicoll to Jess at 12.25 p.m.:

> The Americans have retired from Willow Trench towards F.12 There are some anti-tank guns near the Q. [quarry] in Macquincourt, some more 77s in vicinity of 8d (A.8.d) and there are very large concentrations of M.Gs. in Claymore valley, also big nests of M.Gs. in Bony; Boche still there very thick. Myself and Lamble were actually followed by both artillery and M.G. fire as soon as we started to move. Col. Henderson is killed and Fairweather seriously wounded – Giles is commanding the Bn. Another officer – Callum [Callan]– is lost, killed too.[2]

Fifteen minutes later McNicoll added a most emphatic assessment:

> The 39th have been ordered to stand to. Boche massing on left – Boche is pretty strong down Macquincourt valley in Square 7.a. We have got 39th and 40th there. There are some Americans returning along to the left in about F.12. I don't know where any of 9 Bde . . . On my right the 38th are in 18.c. There are some Yanks in front of them. They are not very far in and not many Yanks. *The line is still held.*[3]

In between these conversations Major Pain, the brigade-major of the 9 Brigade, had spoken to Jess to reaffirm that the situation was as McNicoll stated. Asked by Jess as to where the Americans thought they were, the major replied:

> They believe that one of their battalions went right through the Hindenburg Line, but they have lost them – nothing more is known at all. They don't think

they have a forward line east of that; that is mostly from the wounded, but they won't give it as official.[4]

It was clear to all in the 3rd Division that the Americans had failed and that the incoming Australians were facing a concerted German defence of the outpost line. It would take some time before acknowledgement of this reality penetrated into the next level of command.

Not long after speaking to McNicoll, Jess was briefed by Blamey, Monash's chief of staff, as to how corps was reading the situation. He immediately advised the 11 Brigade commander, General Cannan, of what Blamey had said. Flares had been seen on the Green Line at Guoy, east of Mt St Martin and east of Nauroy. This was held as proof that the Green Line was not only reached but held as well! The assumption that followed was that the Americans had not mopped up and that 'vigorous patrolling' must be undertaken to suppress them. One senses a feeling of incredulity in Cannan's response. He offered up contrary evidence stating:

> Maj. Vasey has been up forward and he got into F. 24 . . . The Boche got two tanks with guns in 14.c. – tank guns, not as big as 77s, but bigger than the anti-tank rifle. There are quite a number of Boche there – there are plenty of Boche in between Bony and the Brown Line.[5]

The divisional commander, John Gellibrand, was also on the ground and he had no doubt as to the severity of the situation. He told Cannan, 'All you can do is hang on.'[6]

It was not long after this that Gellibrand spoke at length with Blamey. The 3rd Division commander stated, 'As far as I can see the Americans have not got their Brown Line,' adding that he thought his men were being asked to do the American's job. Blamey countered, 'No. I think they have got it alright – they have the Green. I think what is wrong is that they have not mopped up.'

Gellibrand then stated that there were not only a number of Americans back with his men but tanks and armoured cars as well. This information clearly rocked Blamey. Gellibrand went on, citing numerous areas in which his men were receiving fire and pointing out that the accuracy of that fire must mean that they were under direct observation from the Germans. Blamey insisted that the Americans were on the Green Line. 'I have not the least doubt about it,' he said. Gellibrand would not be rolled. 'There were planes flying about where I said I was asking for signals', continued the exasperated commander, 'what would they be asking for signals from the Brown Line [start line] for?' Blamey repeated that his information was confirmed from two sources. The two men agreed that the 3rd Division simply had to keep fighting whoever was in their front. Gellibrand spoke of continuing to mop up in concession to the corps view. He pointed out that the operation against the Red Line was ultimately compromised and of the need to send in his reserve brigade. Realisation of the extent of the American disaster seems to have dawned on Blamey by the end of this conversation, 'The fact that the Americans are not on the Green Line is extraordinary.'[7]

The official Australian philosophy remained that the Americans were on the Green Line and that the Australians must push on, mop up and try and make their start line. It was however tacitly understood by all within the 3rd Division that the Americans could not be on the Green. The problem for the Australian commanders was that they could get no agreement from the American personnel that this was in fact the case. The competing strains of American optimism and hard-worn Australian pragmatism were no better illustrated than in a communication from the 27th Division to its corps headquarters:

Am sending a message written by Gen. O'Ryan, which is more or less optimistic. The Australians do not appear well pleased with the situation. They think the battalion which has been reported in Guoy and vicinity have been captured. No confirmation except not hearing from them and a statement from a captured

German officer that they took 700 prisoners. Australian liaison officer states he has received reliable source that the Boche are reinforcing (feeding) men down the road southwest from Catelet to Bony. Australian officer (Salisbury) states there is no chance of those reported in Guoy not being captured.[8]

A priority of the Australian reaction so far had been to form a continuous Australian line free of the straggling and broken elements of the Americans. The 44th Battalion history described the hundreds of Americans with whom they came into contact as being 'utterly demoralised and disorganised' and as having 'lost every atom of cohesion'.[9] The desired independent Australian line was achieved with the linking of the 44th and 58th Battalion. Plans were then put in motion within the 3rd Division to push north along the Hindenburg Line towards the tunnel's northern entrant. The 9 Brigade would be brought in behind the 10 Brigade. It was arranged that the tanks attached to the 9 Brigade would support the 10 Brigade in their advance although it would take two hours before the tanks could get into position.

McNicoll's 10 Brigade was to advance in a northeasterly direction. The 33rd Battalion of Goddard's brigade would attack the Knoll to protect the left flank. The 11 Brigade would protect the right of the 10 Brigade by striking towards the trenches north of Bony. The planned operation was being suggested as one of strong patrolling from corps. However in consulting with his brigadiers Gellibrand placed a greater emphasis than that on the attack. 'Whatever is done will have to be done on a big scale,' he told Cannan.[10]

McNicoll's men were effectively pinned down from fire off the Knoll and from up Claymore valley. They bunkered down in shell holes subject to violent opposition whenever they moved. Their brigadier was not confident about their chances and begrudgingly conceded to the requirement to attack, noting, 'If we have to go, we will go but probably many will not get through.'[11]

The attack was set for 3 p.m. The aim was to move forwards on a broad line and get over the Hindenburg Line making as much progress as possible so as to achieve the best defensive line by nightfall. All straggling Americans were to be stopped from coming back. The attack began as ordered. However it did so without the assistance of either tanks or artillery. The tanks could not reach the infantry in time and the artillery support was withheld because of the uncertainty surrounding the Americans whereabouts.

McNicoll's 10 Brigade rose to their task at 3 p.m. precisely. The 40th Battalion formed the left of the brigade front with the 39th Battalion in the centre and the 38th Battalion on the right. Extending the brigade's left below the Knoll position were various remnants of the earlier American attack. Captain Leland was among them somewhat refreshed after having enjoyed a cigar and some sandwiches.[12] Tactically they would form a defensive flank for McNicoll's men.

As soon as the Australians moved to the attack double red flares rose south of Bony and double green shot up north of the village. A heavy SOS barrage fell immediately on the attacking line. Many German batteries had survived the preliminary bombardments of the previous days because the battery commanders had taken the precaution of moving the battery positions.

The 40th Battalion and the Americans moved by half sections up the hill to the left of Gillemont Farm utilising whatever cover was available. They almost reached Lone Tree Trench when the counterbarrage descended on them forcing them to ground. The men took cover in shell holes and attempted to crawl forwards against the machine-gun fire spitting death from behind a hedge line. At that point they were ordered to abandon the assault.[13] In the centre a similar situation prevailed. The 39th Battalion was occupying the ruins of Gillemont Farm and managed to edge forwards fractionally under heavy fire. The left company under Captain R. Wolstenholme seized a part of South Gillemont Trench.[14]

On the right the 38th Battalion had greater success. It advanced with C and A Companies with many Americans scattered throughout. Thick strands of wire held them up as did the machine-gun and sniper fire that covered the gaps that had been deliberately placed to entice the attackers through. A few tanks had been appropriated to assist the attack but these lasted only a few minutes under the direct fire of the German guns. A smoke barrage was requested to screen the advance of the infantry. This was dropped successfully and skilfully by an aeroplane into Claymore valley. Artillery support also fell on the German line where machine-gun posts had been spotted – clearance for such selective shooting having been granted by the American commanders. Under its cover and with the artillery support, the Australians and Americans were able to get into South Gillemont Trench, which they found devoid of the enemy except for a few wounded men left behind. One section of this trench however was found to be already occupied by Lieutenant Donnecker and forty men of the American 108th Regiment, they having reached it in the morning attack.[15]

After an hour of heavy fighting and little progress, General McNicoll advised Gellibrand that it was impossible to advance against such a strong position. The divisional commander asked that he hang on and look to his right for relief where the 11 Brigade was expected to link up. Soon after the brigadier advised that his battalions had 'done their best to get forward but it is absolute suicide'.[16]

General Cannan's 11 Brigade intended to strike east across the Hindenburg Line with the 41st and 44th Battalions. The 42nd Battalion was to follow them and then bomb northwards along the two main German trenches. However the 41st Battalion was still hung up on the outpost line near Quennet Copse and the 44th Battalion was already embroiled in a bomb fight, having earlier gained a portion of the tunnel line in the southern sector of their line. There the 44th banded with some Americans and fought off two German counterattacks that emanated from reinforcing troops behind Bony. Captain S. R. Warry's company of the 42nd Battalion joined the bomb fight at 3 p.m. It pushed into the line behind the 44th Battalion and worked its way northwards extending the line 300 yards in that direction. It could go no further. The rest of the Battalion stopped in keeping with a cancellation order for the attack, which had not reached Warry and his men. Later an attempt was made to reinforce the front line with the 42nd Battalion but so crowded were the trenches that the Battalion was pulled back into reserve, where the men spent a miserable night in heavy rain under an unceasing shower of machine-gun bullets.[17].

Opposing the Australians and Americans at this point in time were two companies of the 241st Engineers, the 3rd Battalion, 87th Regiment with its 3rd Machine Gun Company and the remnants of 65th Regiment. Also the Alexander Battalion from the 2nd Prussian Guard Division was on its way to reinforce the threatened sector between Bony and Cabaret Farm. This division had been summoned early in the morning and was now just arriving after being transported forward by lorries from Clary five miles away.[18]

The portion of the line held by the 11 Brigade formed a critical juncture in the Australian line. It was here that the 3rd Division right met with the 5th Division left. It was here too where more Americans than anywhere else had succeeded in making some gains. An attempt to get the line forward just below this juncture was arranged. Diggers from 'Pompey' Elliott's 15 Brigade and the mixed commands of doughboys banded together to make an assault on Le Catelet–Nauroy Line. Five Mark V tanks and eight whippets had been collected near the 58th Battalion headquarters behind the tunnel mound. The Australian 14 Field Artillery Brigade provided a thin barrage over a 2,000-yard front behind which the tanks advanced, followed by scouts and then sections of Australian and American infantry in artillery file. The ground was entirely open and as they made for Railway Ridge, on which Le Catelet–Nauroy Line lay, a veritable storm of fire swept them from the north, the west and particularly from the fort at Cabaret Farm. Firing over open sights the German gunners hit all the heavy tanks and half the whippets.

The 58th Battalion on the left was decimated and lost fifty per cent of its men. Irrespective of these terrible losses the men battled on to the German line north of the farm where they gained a foothold assisted by a tank that had scattered the company of 3rd Battalion, 87th Regiment garrisoning the

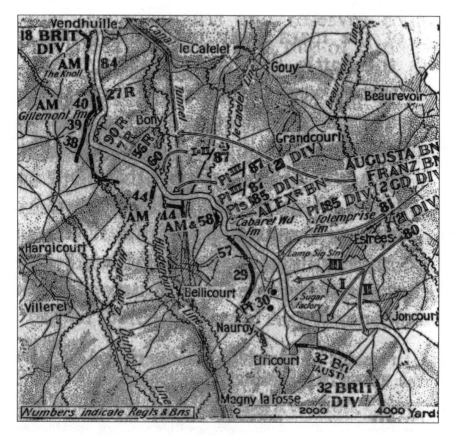

MAP 9 *The Australian–American line showing German positions late afternoon, 29 September*

trenches there.[19] On the right the 57th Battalion used the shelter of the railway embankment to dribble its sections forward. Thus protected they moved around the shoulder of the hill and then by artfully using the depressions of the ground crept up to the German line. They arrived at the 29th Battalion outposts and then bombed northwards along the trenches to a point just south of the Cabaret Farm position. In so doing they drove out the remnants of the 185th Division. These withdrew east to Folemprise Farm where they banded with transport personnel and machine gunners as well as some field guns

111

detached from the 121st Division to form a ragged defensive line. They were soon joined by the Augusta and Franz Battalions of the 2nd Guard Division to bolster the position.[20]

The 57th Battalion's arrival and subsequent success freed up the 29th Battalion, which had been pinned down by the fire from the farm. Thus relieved the 8 Brigade men were able to move forward after dark to take up their position beyond Nauroy, where they relieved the 30th Battalion.[21]

Along Mill Ridge between Folemprise Farm and Joncourt the German 21st Division began to deploy to prevent any further loss of ground. The 81st Regiment was advanced to occupy the Lamp Signal Station, which overlooked Nauroy. The 80th Regiment was sent forward between Estrees and Joncourt to retake Etricourt. In the latter they failed though they occupied the Sugar Factory which lay midway between Estrees and Nauroy. They also claimed to have stopped an enemy advance on Joncourt.[22] This was probably one of the 32nd Battalion patrols sent forward by Wark.

By nightfall the Germans had consolidated their defensive line east of Le Catelet–Nauroy Line and were preparing to defend the area in depth. The 119th Division was brought up by motor transport from Busigny to man the Beaurevoir Line. Along the whole Fourth Army British front the German line ran from Vendhuille to the Knoll down to Gillemont Farm, from there to Bony where it cut back south of the town eastwards over the Hindenburg Line across the exposed slopes to Cabaret Farm. The line started anew at Folemprise Farm extending along Mill Ridge through the towns of Estrees and Joncourt with some advance posts towards Nauroy and Etricourt. From Joncourt the line was shaky with many of the reserves having been trapped in Le Tronquoy tunnel sector by the 46th Division.

The limited success on the Australian–American Corps front was perhaps felt more keenly with the knowledge of the success of the other British armies. Horne's First Army had crossed the Canal du Nord towards Cambrai and penetrated to a distance of four miles beyond its objective. Southwest of Cambrai

Byng's Third Army reached the St Quentin Canal. Further north the Belgian, French and British forces under the command of King Albert of Belgium drove the Germans beyond Passchendaele Ridge and recaptured Messines.

Monash would not have dwelled on these happy outcomes for long. He had work to do and set his mind to organising another assault. The Australian commander still believed the German resistance to be emanating from isolated pockets. Clearly his chief of staff had not been convinced by Gellibrand's argument earlier in the day or, if he had, was unable to sway his commander's opinion. It was around this time that Pasefield's observations were communicated to corps by none other than General Gellibrand. The artillery officer had given an account of his journey to 10 Brigade headquarters. The probable conclusion drawn by Gellibrand that there would now be no Americans left in Guoy was given little weight.[23]

The new plan called for the two divisional reserve brigades to be put into the fight side by side. They were to assemble along the line that connected the two divisions south of Bony. It was here that the Americans of the 108th Regiment had held on throughout the day. The 9 Brigade was to form the left wing attacking northward with a view of taking Bony and the Knoll before moving on to the tunnel entrant. The 14 Brigade would form the right wing and aim for Railway Ridge advancing northeasterly to gain the ridge line running from the Knob around to the Lamp Signal Station near Nauroy. The Australians were to clear the ground gained and link up with the Americans who were presumed to be forward in these areas. Such was the intention when the day closed.[24]

General Monash spoke to Gellibrand in the evening about the plan. 'The Knob is the key to the whole situation', he declared, adding, 'In view of the success in other parts things will be better tomorrow than today.'[25]

At 5 p.m. a miserable drizzling rain set in. The churned-up ground began to turn to mud. Cold and soaked through, the troops huddled in the trenches further chilled by an icy wind, which blustered against them. Gas shells

113

continued to be fired throughout the night forcing the Australians to don their masks in response to the frequent alarms. The hot meals brought to them in the early hours were a warming, if only momentary, balm against the cold on what was remembered as one of the coldest nights in the troops' front-line experience.

CHAPTER NINE

30 September

'We cannot afford to lose a battle because the Americans are supposed to be there.' –
General John Monash

On the evening of 29 September General Monash consulted with his army commander about the progress of the battle and on what to do next. The level of disorganisation in the American divisions meant they were incapable of participating effectively in any more attacks. It was agreed that they be withdrawn from the immediate front and spared further fighting as soon as was practicable.

The anticipated American withdrawal meant that the flanking British Corps would have to take over the tasks that had been allotted to the American divisions previously. On the left the XIII Corps was to relieve the III Corps at midday and take over the northern part of the Australian front from the Knoll and Gillemont Farm sectors. The Australians would continue pushing north to Le Catelet but were also to strike east at the German line stretching from Guoy to Folemprise Farm and Estrees. On the right the British IX Corps would continue to press eastwards with the intention of securing Joncourt, Preselles and Sequehart to open up the approach to the Beaurevoir Line. The 5 Cavalry Brigade was transferred from the Australian Corps to the IX Corps, where it was believed it might have greater opportunity to move.[1]

The German position early on 30 September was much as it had finished the previous evening. The 54th Division held the line from Vendhuille, behind the canal, and the Hindenburg Line from Macquincourt Farm to Bony. A company of the 27th Regiment had been posted at the northern entrance to the tunnel as the Germans feared it might be used as an avenue of attack given the southern entrant had been captured. South of Bony in the Hindenburg Line was the Augusta Battalion, of the 2nd Prussian Guards Division, with two battalions – 1st Battalion, 87th Regiment and 2nd Battalion, 87th Regiment – defending the elbow of the German position where it cut back across the tunnel line. There the 241st Engineers and the Franz Battalion had defensive posts with the latter's line jagging northeastwards up Vauban valley to Railway Ridge, along which ran Le Catelet–Nauroy Line. An advanced battery of the 241st Field Artillery Regiment was pushed up the valley behind the guardsmen. The Alexander Battalion occupied Le Catelet–Nauroy Line and further east across Soult valley lay the 3rd Machine Gun Company and a detachment of the 65th Regiment connecting the line to Cabaret Farm.[2]

One limiting factor in all Allied planning was the artillery restrictions that were imposed. The guns of both Australian divisions were still under battle control of the Americans. As the American commanders still believed or preferred to believe that Americans were on the Green Line objectives the use of heavy artillery along that line was prohibited. In addition, barrages on the Hindenburg Line were limited to only where the Germans were known to be present. Protective creeping barrages, emphatically denied on 29 September, were agreed on at a late hour as being a necessary evil.[3]

The inclement weather that had visited the battlefield now began to wield an influence. At 9.25 p.m. on 29 September Brigadier-General Goddard had advised 3rd Division HQ that he needed seven clear hours to make the 12,500-yard march overnight to reach his brigade's allocated start position and that he doubted if his men would get to the line at zero hour.[4] This information was communicated to corps and a new plan quickly formulated. The 3rd Division would continue to fight its way forwards with the 10 Brigade on the left or northern section of the line. It was arranged for the 11 Brigade to attack in conjunction up the Hindenburg Line towards Bony and then east towards

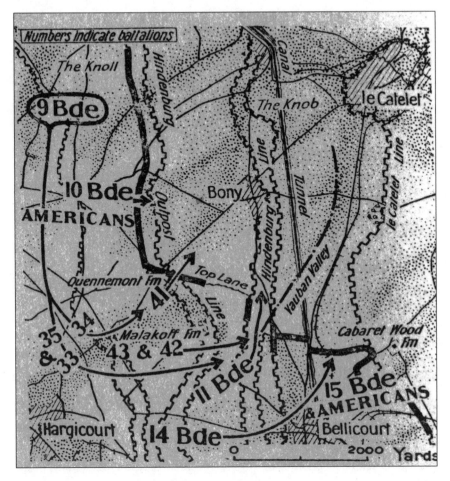

MAP 10 *Realignment of the Australian and American line, 30 September*

Le Catelet–Nauroy Line. The 41st Battalion would hold the left of the brigade front with the 44th, 42nd and 43rd Battalions leapfrogging through each other in successive bounds as part of the main attack. Goddard's 9 Brigade would move to a position east of Malakoff Farm where its 34th Battalion would join with the 41st Battalion, temporarily under 9 Brigade command, and clear the outpost line. The 33rd and 35th Battalions were to sweep southwards and come in behind the 11 Brigade to support its attack. The 14 Brigade was next in line and would attack north and east to seize the section of Le Catelet–Nauroy Trench line on its front. The 15 Brigade on its right and already in Le Catelet–Nauroy Line would shift its garrison north and then relieve the 14 Brigade and continue the attack eastwards.[5] Zero hour for 30 September was set at 7 a.m. as the infantry commanders wanted better light in which to work.

In view of the minimal artillery protection that was ultimately given, an attempt was made to provide some tanks to support the attacking infantry. Communications however quickly broke down. One of the corps terminal poles was knocked over by a tank around midnight, which contributed to the loss of communication. During the night, in the inky blackness, the infantry guides for tanks and infantrymen alike became hopelessly lost.

Major Merritt of the 13th Tank Battalion had received his orders to move late the previous evening in support of the forthcoming attack. He had worked hard through the night to get his men and machines in position. He drew up on the start line at 6.50 a.m. southwest of Bony, alongside the main road into the town. He had six tanks in position plus another of the 16th Battalion. The Australian infantry whom the tanks were to accompany were nowhere to be seen. Merritt decided to start without them. The tanks moved forwards under a desultory fire until they got close to Bony, where considerable machine-gun and anti-tank fire was directed at them. Undaunted Merritt took the tanks past the village, successfully disposing of some of the troublesome posts. He continued on with the mission along the western edge of the German defences up towards the northern tunnel entrant near Vendhuille. The tanks encountered little opposition and by noon had returned to their rallying point east of Hargicourt. As the author of the history of the 13th Tank Battalion suggested, 'such piratical expeditions of tanks without escort cannot be upheld as a model of tank tactics'. The combination of relief and bemusement was captured succinctly by one of the participating tank men, 'We walked down the Hindenburg Line, but luckily Hindenburg was not at home.'[6]

The tanks' journey revealed the glad news of the morning, confirmed by various infantry patrols later on, that the Germans had vacated Gillemont Farm as well as Vendhuille Trench and the village itself. Without the protective benefit of these positions the defence of the Knoll could not be maintained and it was necessarily abandoned. The abandonment of the remaining sector of the outpost line was in keeping with new German policy formulated by Hindenburg in response to the massive attacks that had lately been directed against the German armies. The costly policy of immediate counterattack to regain lost ground, now made nearly impossible by a lack of reserves, was replaced by one of considered withdrawal and the defence of pivotal points in the main line.[7] This shift merely reiterated the initial expectation of the defence of the outpost line in the Bellicourt sector.

On the far left of the line, patrols from the British 18th Division pushed up to the canal but could not cross it. Snipers and machine-gun posts on the opposite side still made passage of the waterway an extremely hazardous venture. Thereabouts Captain R. A. Chell, brigade major of the 55 Brigade, happened on a group of fifty to sixty leaderless Americans. On being asked what they should do he suggested, probably in fairly prosaic terms, that getting on with the war was a good start. Moving forwards Chell came on the bodies of a number of Americans near Vendhuille. A boastful note was left by the Germans in an abandoned machine-gun post, 'Dear Tommy – from this place I shot sixty American soldiers with my machine gun; they came like sheeps [sic]'.[8] Large clusters of American dead were noted by the incoming troops all along the line, proof of the difficulties and hardship they had encountered on approaching the German defences.

The 6th Buffs, which had occupied the most forward positions in the 12th Division's sector, now went forward with the left of the 18th Division into the western outskirts of Vendhuille. Some confusion ensued when a tank suddenly began to fire on them. It was probably one of Cutler's 'piratical' band or otherwise a single machine that had pushed up in support of the remnants of the American line on the Australian left. Company Sergeant Major J. Smith rushed up to the bothersome machine and beat on the front plate with his rifle and quickly gained the attention of the crew thus averting a complete disaster.[9]

At Gillemont Farm patrols from the Australian 10 Brigade found the outpost line abandoned leaving only the German and American dead of the previous fighting. The 40th Battalion formed its headquarters in Willow Trench, leaving its reserve company at Gillemont Farm. The other three companies occupied Gillemont Crescent and Lone Tree Trench. The left thus connected with the English and Americans to the north and its right linked with the 39th Battalion.[10] Patrols from the 37th Battalion occupied the Knoll and went forward towards Vendhuille, which was being shelled heavily by the German guns on the opposite side of the canal. There they made contact with advanced posts of the 6th Northamptons, the 8th East Surrey and Royal Fusilier regiments.[11]

From the newly gained positions patrols felt their way cautiously across the ground towards Bony. Claymore Trench was cleared and a machine-gun post captured. The Germans had taken four Hotchkiss guns from a disabled tank to set up the troublesome post.[12] Captain Peters led a company of the 38th Battalion down Bony Avenue with one patrol reaching the slope below the town. However fire from the area was still too hot to maintain any position for long and so the Australian gains were minimal. In fact any approach from half a mile distance was immediately met with machine-gun fire. Southwest of the town the 34th Battalion cleared some of the German defenders from Dirk valley but they too were held up by heavy defensive fire.[13]

The 41st Battalion was holding Quennemont Farm, where it waited for the 34th Battalion to join it. From here the Australian line doglegged eastwards along Top Lane, the western end being held by them, into the main Hindenburg Line. Much of the wire in this area was still uncut, leaving an impenetrable tangle before the attacking troops. It was from the main trench of the Hindenburg Line leading up to the German occupied portion of Top

Lane that the 11 Brigade attack was to be launched. The 44th Battalion had been ordered to lead the assault but when the barrage opened at 6 a.m. they, wet through and exhausted from the previous day's fighting, had not yet received the order. Similarly the 42nd Battalion, which was to pass through the 44th Battalion, did not receive its orders until 8 a.m. An advanced platoon of that battalion was rudely surprised by the barrage falling on it near Top Lane. Further back in Triangle Trench west of Quennemont Farm the 42nd Battalion set off at 3.30 a.m. in the rain and dark to fulfil its end of the bargain. They were thankful to be leaving the area as it was thick with Australian and American dead. Before doing so though many of the men souvenired the American corpses taking money and whatever other valuables they felt were of more use to the living.[14] The 42nd Battalion arrived at about 7 a.m. and with the 44th Battalion bombed a German post out of Top Lane.[15]

Apart from the dark and slippery conditions encountered during the night one of the contributing factors to the late orders was the congestion met with by the runners. A dense mass of troops had accumulated in the gully which ran behind Top Lane down to Malakoff Farm Woods. The front trenches were crammed to overflowing with Americans and men of the 42nd and 44th Battalion. Behind them tanks and the troops of three other battalions left little room for manoeuvre. Such was the level of congestion that the incoming 35th Battalion was withdrawn until the area cleared sufficiently.[16]

By mid-morning things were manageable and at 11 a.m. Captain Moran arrived with the 43rd Battalion and cleared Top Lane completely of Germans. This allowed his companies to push up both Hindenburg trenches towards Bony. This was attempted but further advance was rendered impossible by the fire from Bony and Le Catelet–Nauroy Line east of it.[17] During this action in a tragic sidelight, a German shell brought to an end, in one fell swoop, the life of that battalion's only Victoria Cross winner, Lance Corporal Lawrence Carthage Weathers, and his uncle and brother-in-arms Lance-Corporal J. J. Weathers.[18]

The 14 Brigade attack began a little behind schedule. It was 500 yards short of the start line when the support barrage descended. The brigade commander, Lieutenant-Colonel Cheeseman, led the men forward personally – there being no guides available who knew the way. The men had had a difficult night trying to organise into their companies in the early hours. The supporting artillery brigades – the 13th and 14th Australian Field Artillery – were also placed under a severe strain. They received their orders at 3 a.m. and 1 a.m., respectively, and it was a taxing task to swing the guns around in the dark and gain the correct bearings. They also had to bring up ammunition for the guns, which in the conditions was extremely tiring. As a consequence the barrage – already reduced from three rounds a minute to one – was considered relatively light by the men who were to advance under its cover.[19]

The intention of the barrage was to protect the flank of the advancing infantry. The problem for the 14 Brigade was that as its left flank swung eastwards it became increasingly exposed to the Germans in Bony and the areas to the north and east. With the 9 and 10 Brigade unable to pass Bony this was to have a most deleterious effect on the exposed infantrymen. The left companies of the 53rd Battalion, which were leading the advance, suffered heavy casualties and sought shelter along the eastern face of the tunnel line. That protected them from fire from Bony and the main Hindenburg Line but not from that coming down the Vauban valley and off the ridge, where Le Catelet–Nauroy Line lay east of them. Nevertheless some gains were made by the right companies. Captain C. A. Jhonson with his men entered Le Catelet system and drove the Germans back 300 yards before they rallied and counterattacked. Seeing this and being under heavy fire in their current position, Captain Wilson led his men off the mound and struck the Germans in the flank. Wilson was killed but in combination with those under Jhonson, who was later mortally wounded, his men forced the Germans further northwards in desperate fighting.[20]

Behind them Lieutenant R. V. Hill of the support company inherited the same problem. With six men he worked along the tunnel mound seizing one post manned by twenty Germans with three machine guns and then overcame another post set in a dugout. However a strongpoint beyond those could not be conquered. Like the other companies, Hill's company was ironically driven east into Le Catelet–Nauroy Line. There he led numerous attacks to extend the line a further 600 yards northwards. The Germans he faced most likely belonged to the Alexander Battalion. Their retreat northwards exposed the flank of the 3rd Battalion, 87th Regiment enabling Lieutenant Ralph to lead his company stealthily eastwards from Le Catelet–Nauroy trenches. Ralph managed to infiltrate behind the German lines to the headquarters of 3rd Battalion, 87th Regiment situated in Soult valley. There Captain Hoyer, the battalion commander, was startled by machine-gun bullets skimming across his dugout entrance. Seeing the way barred by the enemy working up from the south he destroyed all his papers and then ordered his men, numbering about forty, to surrender. Unfortunately Ralph was mortally wounded during the journey back.[21]

Lying across the tunnel line was the 55th Battalion. On its left in Tunnel Sap was a body of Americans from the American 118th and 119th Regiments, some of whom had acted as carriers bringing up vital supplies of ammunition and rations for the attacking diggers.[22] The doughboys extended the line west to link with the 44th Battalion in Top Lane and the first or western trench of the Hindenburg Line. Some of the 55th Battalion had advanced along the tunnel line in response to a call for assistance from the 53rd Battalion but there ran into the same heavy fire as they descended the slope towards Bony that had foiled the earlier efforts. They too were driven off by trench mortars and took refuge in Le Catelet–Nauroy Line.[23]

While the battle raged in this area, events of interest were occurring in the tunnel itself. Lieutenant L. S. Brown, the gas officer of the 8 Brigade, had established his headquarters at the tunnel's southern entrant. At its mouth a number of German dead lay on stretchers, wounded who had either been left unattended or who had been killed by artillery fire. Inside the tunnel mouth a shell had killed many of the occupants and upended one unfortunate fellow into a vat of water used for cooking or laundry most probably. This gruesome finding had given rise to a wild rumour that the Germans were boiling human bodies down for fat. The story appeared in Australian diaries within twenty-four hours and was being quickly communicated around the world by war correspondents as an example of the unfathomable depths of German perfidy.

In the afternoon Brown decided to explore the tunnel. Alone he moved north to a spot below Bellicourt. Proceeding a little further he could hear machine-gun fire above him. He found an exit that led to a passageway of a shelter that was crowded with Americans. The doughboys had not realised that their position connected with the tunnel. The commanding officer present detailed two officers to accompany Brown while he continued his inspection. Continuing on they saw a flickering of light that marked the northern entrance. The closer they crept the larger loomed the light. Suddenly all was dark and the noise of an explosion barrelled down the tunnel towards them. The three were bowled over by the concussion of what they believed to be a mine. Picking themselves up, they ran for the safety of daylight at the southern end, fearing that other mines might soon be detonated. At the German end the torchlight of Brown's party had been spotted by the engineers causing them hastily to collapse the tunnel entrant. Tragically for the company of the 27th Regiment guarding the entrant it was not informed and suffered unnecessary and grievous loss.[24]

Early in the afternoon the Germans mounted a two-prong counterattack to try to win back Le Catelet–Nauroy Line. They worked their way south down the trenches and drove the defending Australians back a considerable distance. At the same time they attacked across the open ground to the east of Le Catelet–Nauroy Line. A spirited defence by Private John Ryan of the 55th Battalion averted further inroads being made. He organised a few men and rushed forwards to disperse the threat on the front before counterattacking up the trenches to regain some of the lost ground.[25]

The failure of the 14 Brigade to advance further eastwards meant the 15 Brigade could not shift northwards to man the trenches behind it. Pompey Elliott's brigade did not remain idle. It probed forwards with patrols to feel out the Cabaret Farm position, which was found to be still occupied by about forty Germans with machine guns.[26]

Further south along the slopes beyond Nauroy lay the 8 Brigade stretching across the valley to Etricourt and connecting with the British 32nd Division's left flank. Here Wark's 32nd Battalion continued to enjoy success on the far right. The left of the brigade however was overlooked by Germans holding the high ground ahead between the Lamp Signal Station and the Sugar Factory, the line that had been organised the previous night. After a number of earlier failures to carry the line forward, the 29th Battalion arranged to attack at 4 p.m. with the assistance of some heavy artillery. The barrage was ineffective and actually fell behind the flanks of the 29th Battalion. On its left the 57th Battalion of the 15 Brigade tried to assist. Neither could make headway. Any further attempts were branded suicidal and the attack was promptly halted.[27]

On the British IX Corps front the success of the previous day was stymied somewhat by greater German resistance. On the right Le Tronquoy tunnel line was mopped up completely and the village of Levergies was captured. However on the left neither Sequehart nor Joncourt was able to be subdued. Working in conjunction with the British 32nd Division, Wark's 32nd Battalion pushed its line nearly a thousand yards east towards Joncourt drawing up about three hundred yards southwest of the village.[28]

That evening orders were issued to the Australian commanders to return all Americans attached to their units with the exception of any required for garrison duty. The doughboys near the Knoll remained but by dawn most Americans had been withdrawn, thus ending their contribution to the battle for the Hindenburg Line.[29] The gains made on 30 September and the severity of the fighting demonstrated unequivocally that the opposition was more than 'isolated pockets' and that more hard fighting would likely be required on the morrow to force the Germans back.

Monash's irritation with the progress of the battle came to the fore in an insensitive denunciation of his 3rd Division commander's tactics that evening. Why, he asked, had Gellibrand attacked on so narrow a front? Gellibrand pointed out that the line strength of his battalions were little more than 200 effectives. Monash scotched this truth claiming some battalions were 600 strong insinuating that Gellibrand's estimation was effectually nonsense. Why, persisted the corps commander, was the division committed on such a narrow front? Gellibrand, by now somewhat incensed, replied pointedly that having visited the front line it was his assessment that he could make no further advance at the present time.

Ironically Monash concluded the conversation by echoing Gellibrand's assessment of the previous day about the unlikelihood of any Americans being beyond the Hindenburg Line. He urged his divisional commander to use his artillery freely, Gellibrand having been previously constrained by O'Ryan's concern for the safety of alleged detached outlying American troops:

> There cannot be any Americans east of you. They must be either prisoners or strafed. Anyway we cannot afford to lose a battle because the Americans are supposed to be there.[30]

Monash's irritation with the American effort by this time had developed into a feeling of entrenched disgust. It was the Australian general's opinion that their performance completely vindicated his worst fears. That evening he spoke with Charles Bean, the official war correspondent, and unburdened himself, 'Well, you see what I expected might happen has happened. The Americans sold us a pup. They're simply unspeakable.'[31]

CHAPTER TEN

The Last Ridge

'Damn it, if you can do it, do it now!' – Pompey Elliott, Australian brigadier

The first day of the new month of October dawned grey and misty. The rain that had drenched the soldiers for a second consecutive night had eased to a drizzle. The withdrawal of the Americans removed the concern held for any survivors along the Green Line. Monash, whose patience had been severely tried by the greenness of the doughboys, now resolved to launch a frontal assault supported by a heavy barrage. The 3rd Division would strike east at the Germans in the Hindenburg Line and the 5th Division, with its left anchored in Le Catelet–Nauroy Line, would strike northeast at Railway Ridge and Mill Ridge. The corps boundary was marked as the northern tunnel entrant on the left, and on the right the village of Joncourt marked the southernmost point. On gaining this line the 5th Division was to exploit as far as possible towards the Beaurevoir Line.[1]

Having endured two days of heavy fighting, the commander of the 3rd Division was not well disposed to his commander's plan. Gellibrand spoke directly with Monash early in the morning and succeeded in dissuading him from launching what amounted to a frontal attack. Instead the 3rd Division would revert to its method of the previous days of trying to work up the Hindenburg Line and turn the German flank at Bony. Ten tanks from the 16th Tank Battalion were attached to the 10 Brigade to assist in taking the town.[2]

Bearing in mind the flare-up between the two the previous day, this morning's conversation was an indication that Monash had regained some of his composure and battlefield logic. He apologised to Gellibrand for his attitude and later wrote positively, though somewhat guardedly, of Gellibrand's contribution to the victory. Describing the 3rd Division commander as 'more a philosopher and a student than a man of action' and as one whose temperament was prone to involve him in administrative embarrassments, Monash went on to state:

> I feel certain from my close observation of the course of events on 30 September and 1 October that much of the success of the battle was due to Gellibrand's personal tenacity and the assiduous manner in which he kept himself in personal touch from hour to hour with the forward situation and progress of his troops.[3]

This concession suggests Monash may have been sensitive to Gellibrand's jibe that, in response to his commander's misguided demands, he had arrived at his conclusions by visiting the front. The shame was that Monash's postwar observation of his subordinate's method had not been appreciated fully at the time.

During the night the Germans had withdrawn east towards the Beaurevoir Line. The German withdrawal had offered hitherto unseen opportunities. The tired eyes of the Australian and British artillerymen were brightened by the sight of undamaged country and postcard perfect villages behind the Hindenburg Line.[4]

The day's barrage opened at 6am. Under its cover, patrols pushed forward all along the line to find only small numbers of Germans holding the previous strongpoints. The German line was now configured thus. The villages of Le Catelet and Guoy were held by the 54th Division and the 87th Regiment. The 2nd Prussian Guard Division and the 119th Division now manned the main trench line west of Beaurevoir. The 21st Division lay west of Estrees and the

241st Division west of Joncourt. This marked the left boundary of General von Carlowitz's Second Army. Further south at Sequehart in the British sector was the 34th Division of the German Eighteenth Army.[5]

The extreme left of the Australian line was held by the 37th Battalion with the 40th on its right and the 39th further south. After establishing that the Hindenburg Line had been cleared, patrols from these battalions of the 3rd Division began pushing east at 11 a.m. Artillery on the slopes northwest of Le Catelet kept up a heavy fire with the gunners sniping over open sights at the various patrols of Australians working forwards. The line was advanced 400 yards with the left anchored in Knob Wood then stretching south to Bony Point. At the Knob the 37th Battalion found the trenches packed with German dead. Strewn before the position were the lifeless forms of many Americans who had clearly got through the outpost line on 29 September only to be cut down in front of the broad trenches of the Hindenburg Line.[6]

In the evening patrols from the 40th Battalion explored Macquincourt Farm behind Knob Wood. Opposite the farm on the other side of the canal they could hear the Germans talking in the trenches.[7] Other than that all was quiet in the Hindenburg Line, where exhausted Australian soldiers welcomed the protection and drying comfort of the deep concrete caverns previously occupied by their enemy.

In marked contrast to the previous day's fighting the 5th Division was on its objective by 7.30 a.m. Lieutenant-Colonel Denehy of the 57th Battalion advised 15 Brigade headquarters that his men were on the objective and, though very tired, could probably push on. Pompey Elliott was quick to exhort him to do so, 'Damn it, if you can do it, do it now!'[8] Patrols were pushing forward by 9 a.m. For a time parties operating around Estrees, Mint Copse and Folemprise Farm came under direct fire from the German guns that were now setting up on the slopes behind the new German line. Prompt counterbattery fire soon relieved the situation.

On the right flank Wark's depleted companies of the 32nd Battalion were finally relieved by a company of the 30th Battalion. The 30th Battalion had been designated as the brigade reserve. One company was in line, another was sent to support the 31st Battalion and the third sent to relieve the 32nd Battalion. The approach march of the latter company had not been a happy one and they arrived in bad humour. They had endured a night of constantly changing bivouacs to avoid gas shelling. Their uniforms reeked from clinging gas and with their gas masks donned they looked like 'goblin monks'. When they received the order to move, it was initially welcomed as it freed them from the 'pestilential area' in which they had been camped. They were then forced march through 'an oily black night of slanting rain' during which they had 'to weave through a tangle of rusty wire and murky shell holes, and gyrate over much smelly battle debris'. Near Magny la Fosse they were sprayed by machine-gun fire that covered the ground over which they had to pass. Forced to earth by this fire they prostrated themselves in the mud and belly crawled and tobogganed themselves from one slimy shell hole to the next.[9]

One among them was Private G. V. Rose. He admitted to being considerably disgusted by the move, a sentiment not helped by his spilling half his rum issue in the dark. Rose had found a snug and safe 'possie' underneath a viaduct where the Nauroy road intersected the railway line. He had to abandon this for the night march and set off with his swearing and cursing mates into the dark. Finally they arrived, dog tired, in the vicinity of Etricourt to the delight of the remnants of Wark's command. As dawn broke they stumbled forward behind the morning's barrage and followed it up to Mill Ridge, which was promptly abandoned by the Germans.[10]

The men could not remain on the exposed slopes of Mill Ridge for long, and so in keeping with the orders to exploit forwards they with the 32nd Battalion in support continued the attack towards the picturesque village of Joncourt. The village was captured shortly after 10 a.m., from which point it was shelled by the unsentimental German gunners. The gay red tiled roofs

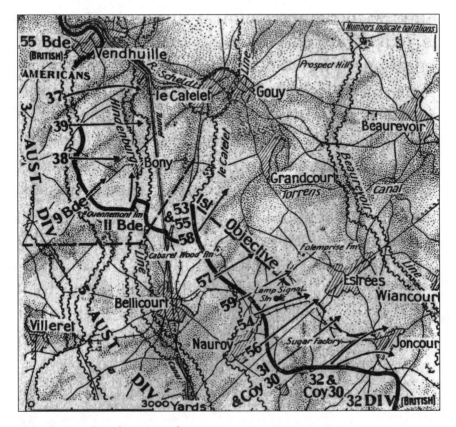

MAP II *Australian advance 1 October*

and undamaged green hedges were suddenly subject to a heavy bombardment. Gas shells drenched the town seeping into the cellars where the Australians had sought cover. The church spire was unceremoniously snapped by one incoming salvo. Emboldened the Germans rushed up a battery of guns close to the town's outskirts and began a duel with the Lewis gunner posts that had been set up. They took out one post but fell in turn to the daisy-cutting fire unleashed by the Australian Lewis gunners who responded to the challenge.[11]

The Australians had entered the village as the Germans were debouching from the other end in lorries. The retreating Germans headed down the slope to Wiancourt and to Beaurevoir on the hill behind. From Joncourt the Australians sniped at the Germans in the distance, who in turn kept a lively fire on the village with machine guns and artillery. An enemy plane took an interest in the affair and swept over the Australians before being driven off by Lewis gunners firing off the shoulders of their No. 2s.[12] When the 17th Battalion arrived to relieve the 30th Battalion, Private G. V. Rose was certainly one who was 'anxious to get out of it' particularly as there was a pervading sense that it might be the unit's last turn in the trenches.[13]

By nightfall the 5th Division had exploited to a position that ran along the Grand Court–Estrees road between Mt St Martin (where American flares had supposedly been seen on 29 September) to Estrees. That evening the relieving units of the Australian 2nd Division began to arrive. The 5th Division had made it 'to the last ridge', a landmark enshrined in W. H. Downing's book of that title.

The tunnel line had been conquered and the Australian line stretched from the northern tunnel entrant, from the Knob along Railway Ridge to Mill Ridge in a line east of Estrees and Joncourt, where they linked with the British 32nd Division. During the night patrols entered Le Catelet and found it abandoned. The Germans facing the Australians in this sector had withdrawn to a line that ran from Aubencheul in the north down to the Beaurevoir Line, which would become synonymous with the 2nd Division's last days.

Now began the 3rd and 5th Divisions' withdrawal from the front line. Both divisions, depleted when the battle had commenced, had lost heavily. The 3rd Division suffered 1,065 casualties and the 5th Division 1,508.[14] The fatigue on the men was patent to everyone and their 'strained, pallid' faces were signal enough for the drivers of incoming transports to pull aside in 'mute and eloquent testimony' to allow the war weary infantrymen to pass.[15] The 3rd and 5th Divisions marched rearwards oblivious to the fact that their war was now over.

The Bellicourt Tunnel battle had turned into a stiffer fight than either Monash or his army commander, Rawlinson, had expected. Contrary to all expectations the Germans had fought surprisingly well. For Monash and the Australians there remained one last act in the sector over which they had just fought. This was the attack on the town of Montbrehain, which was carried out by the 6 Brigade of Major-General Charles Rosenthal's 2nd Division as part of operations during the Battle of the Beaurevoir Line from 3 to 5 October.

Having relieved the 3rd and 5th Divisions, Rosenthal's division, with the Australian 7 Brigade forming the left and the Australian 5 Brigade its right, pushed the line forward between the towns of Beaurevoir and Montbrehain. Like Bony and Bellicourt in the previous days, these two towns were stoutly defended and acted as two strongpoints in this sector of the German line. The British XIII and IX Corps operated on the left and right of the Australians respectively. The 46th Division held Montbrehain for a time before a German counterattack dislodged them.

On 5 October the Australian 6 Brigade captured Montbrehain in a courageous but expensive assault. That evening the 2nd Division was relieved by troops from the American II Corps. The doughboys were now operating autonomously with the Australian field artillery attached. The Australian artillery brigades remained with Fourth Army as it pushed on to the Selle river, supporting both British and American divisions. By mid-October the Germans were on the back foot on all fronts. In the south the French–American Meuse–Argonne offensive had pushed the Germans back on the vital Mezieres–Montmedy rail line. In Flanders King Albert's British–Belgian force reclaimed the Ypres Ridge and pushed beyond the Lys river towards the Dutch border. To the north of Rawlinson's Fourth Army, Byng's Third Army pushed forward from Cambrai to the Selle river.

The depleted Australian divisions were dispatched to quiet sectors well away from the front. The many villages around Abbeville and southwest of Amiens became home for the ragged Australian battalions as they recuperated and followed the news of the Allied advance. On 8 November the Australians were again summoned to move to the front line. The various Australian divisions began to entrain for the front but on 11 November the guns fell silent as the armistice took effect. The war was over.

Conclusion

Giving consideration to the overarching aims of the strategic battle, the Germans came closer to achieving their goals at Bellicourt Tunnel than did their opponents. Though they were driven out of their great bastion, the Hindenburg Line, they prevented the decisive breakthrough that Haig was looking for on the British Fourth Army front. Compared to the reverses suffered in the days prior to 29 September in Foch's grand offensive the Germans had held their ground admirably in this sector. If the Bellicourt Tunnel battle was viewed as a boxing match then the bout could well have been adjudged a draw. In the early sparring the Germans had counterpunched with aplomb. They were then rocked by a huge right hook in the guise of the British IX Corps' success – especially the 46th Division's – that threatened to put them down for the count. However although staggered and forced to concede much ground on the IX Corps front they boxed on doggedly forcing their opponent to a virtual standstill in a vicious slugfest in front of Bony and along the outpost line. The last rounds were spent back pedalling to prevent their opponent landing a further heavy blow. The Germans would have been well pleased with the tactical dexterity they exhibited on the Australian–American front, yet despite their local success the battle, along with the other Allied success, marked the inevitability of an imminent German defeat.

As with most great battles in history certain stories and assumptions characterise the telling. Despite the diligent work of some historians, whose efforts to explore these things often reveal contrary evidence to the popular version, it is the popular which appeals and prevails. This is certainly true of the American and Australian story at the Hindenburg Line. For Americans in the immediate postwar years and since, it was a measure of pride to be able to say that they had broken through the much-vaunted Hindenburg Line. Breakthrough is certainly too grand a word to apply to the limited success achieved by relatively few Americans during the battle. It should also be remembered that the Hindenburg Line was not the American objective but rather Le Catelet–Nauroy Line east of it – the Green Line – that the doughboys were asked to capture. There is no doubt that some small groups of Americans got to and even moved beyond the Green Line in the early morning phase of the battle. Although all were ultimately captured or wiped out, the reports of their success were to have a profound effect on the conduct of the battle.

Understandably American accounts tried to put the best possible slant on their performance. In the 27th Division sector only one battalion could claim to have gained the Hindenburg Line, where it hung on until the reinforcing Australians reached it. This was the American 3rd Battalion, 108th Regiment which gained a section of the main trenches south of Bony. On the 30th Division front limited success was gained in three portions of the line. The most clean-cut of these was the capture of the southern entrant of the Bellicourt Tunnel. Southeast of Bellicourt a few hundred doughboys got through the Hindenburg Line only to become pinned down along the road to Nauroy. A similar number managed to get through the Hindenburg Line just north of Bellicourt before becoming trapped against the railway ridge in front of Le Catelet–Nauroy Line defences.

That the incoming Australians were not happy with the performance of the Americans – from General John Monash down to the lowliest private – would be an understatement. Monash's rage at times appears to have been incandescent. He was ungenerous in his treatment of his allies' failure both at the time and in his postwar utterances. At least the Australian rank and file, who bore witness to the lanes of doughboys slain before the thick belts of German wire, was more charitable and unequivocally acknowledged the bravery of the Americans as well as their obvious rawness.

The greenness of the American divisions was certainly understood by the higher British commanders. The question remains did they do enough to compensate for it in their battle planning? The answer to that must be that they did not. In this, their first major mistake appears to have been an underestimation of the morale of the Germans. It might be argued that the ease in which many war-weary Germans surrendered during the fighting from August onwards justified such thinking. This is true to a point. However the Germans had given notice, in the sector against which the Americans were being asked to attack, that they would not be brushed aside easily. The failure of the British III Corps to gain the Hindenburg outpost line, and thus the designated start line for the main American attack, should have been considered more thoughtfully. It would appear that, instead of a real appreciation being made of the difficulties that it had faced, the failure was attributed to poor command and exhausted troops. To ask an untried American regiment, albeit a super-sized one compared to the British equivalent, to carry out a crucial preliminary operation against a position of such strength was to ask too much.

Ideally the III Corps should have been bolstered and ordered to carry the outpost line. Failing that another option was to bring up seasoned troops such as the Australian 2nd Division, it being the Australian Corps reserve division for the forthcoming attack. This would have been preferable to using up troops that, if successful, then had to participate in the main attack. One reason why Monash did not offer or consider offering the Australian 2nd Division to undertake the preliminary operation might have been that such a demand could have added fuel to the already inflammatory condition of his own corps' morale. The threat of a general strike or mutiny within Australian ranks was certainly something that required a cautious approach given the open dissatisfaction being aired by some battalions towards imagined excessive workloads and very real threats of disbandment.

The blame for the initial American failure must lie chiefly with Field-Marshal Haig and Rawlinson. Haig, who wanted to preserve the doughboys for the main attack, should not have allowed Rawlinson to convince him otherwise. Rawlinson should have been more circumspect in his viewing of the reasons behind the III Corps' failure but seems to have been moved by frustration at its lack of progress up to that point in time.

As the Americans were under the Australian general's direct command Monash too must shoulder some of the blame. While he was happy to secure the American attachment knowing their large size would bolster his corps and provide welcome relief for his exhausted Australian troops, he was also responsible for the Americans' immediate welfare. The formulation of the Australian mission to assist with the prebattle planning and organisation was a positive step in that regard, though it is difficult to judge its effectiveness given the general failure of the American attack. Nevertheless that aside Monash did not integrate the Americans sufficiently in his own mind when it came to fighting the battle – he viewed them as a separate entity and not his own. Consequently he allowed the preliminary battle to be played out with the allocated resources without intervention.

Given the importance of the attack in securing the start line for the main operation one would have thought Monash would have taken a keener personal interest in its outcome. Instead, beyond having allocated a support battalion to the attack prior to the battle, he let the operation run its course under the auspices of a patently inexperienced American command. Had Monash applied himself to a more critical analysis of the events that were unfolding he may have chanced a bolstering of the attacking line at the critical moment on the afternoon of 27 September, which may have succeeded in carrying the outpost line. These things are of course easily said with hindsight.

That said the preliminary attack on 27 September was well supported with artillery and tanks. It was relatively successful in the first stage in that the attacking battalions at least got to grips with the enemy at all the strongpoints, even breaking through for a time on the Knoll. Had a strong reinforcement been sent up to the line hard on the heels of the first attacking troops the position may have been gained or a foothold obtained closer to the intended jump-off line. The 27th Division's commander, General John O'Ryan, believed that had the 54 Brigade been thrown into a night attack on 27/28 September it 'would have overcome the fatigued German survivors of the day's battle'.[1] O'Ryan does not appear to have tried to impress this view on Monash during the crucial time in which such a decision was needed. Had Monash adopted a more hands-on approach it may have been considered. Unfortunately the Australian general did not have his finger on the pulse of the battle at that early stage. However Monash's mindset – a mirror to Haig's – was to preserve as much of the American force as possible for the main strike. The consequence of this was that the American 106th Regiment was left to fight alone with little support. It further underscores the preference for the use of a different formation that could have utilised its whole strength, such as the Australian 2nd Division.

The failure to take the outpost line during the preliminary operation irrevocably derailed the Fourth Army battle plan. It shouldn't have. When the likelihood that the start line for 29 September was not going to be obtained, Monash asked for a postponement of the main operation to allow extra time for the ground to be carried. Had this been done, hundreds of lives would have been saved. Instead it was decided that the 27th Division would have to commence its attack an hour early on 29 September to make up the 1,000 yards needed to get them to the start line.

The main argument against the postponement was that the Fourth Army was locked into the plan for successive hammer blows, which Field-Marshal Foch and his senior commanders thought would overwhelm the German

Army. With the success of the first three strikes Rawlinson was doubtless anxious to get things rolling on his own front. It is difficult to see how a delay of a day or even two would have had any negative effect on the operation or the grand strategic outcome. The Germans were hard pressed on their other fronts and could ill afford to siphon off forces from those areas to the Bellicourt Tunnel sector or anywhere else for that matter. Nor could they weaken the tunnel sector while under threat of imminent attack. A postponement could only have been beneficial to the Fourth Army assault.

The one factor that nobody had predicted was the thickness of the fog that descended over the battlefield at the appointed hour. Soldiers from both sides fought virtually blind for the first two hours. It was the attacking troops who benefited most from this mist in the initial stage. It was an invaluable shield that allowed them to avoid the direct fire that might otherwise have been brought against them. However it was not without its drawbacks. Keeping one's line and bearings were difficult at the best of times when under enemy fire but even more so in an impenetrable mist. Even during the successful 8 August operation where fog had also screened the Fourth Army assault, the attacking troops became entangled and lost and tanks did not make the start line. Spear-heading that assault were the veteran, if not elite, Canadian and Australian Corps supported by a well-executed artillery bombardment. Those experienced troops pushed on adapting to the situation as required. Critically the American inexperience and the lack of an adequate supporting barrage on the 27th Division front and the failure of the bombardment to destroy the German wire on parts of the 30th Division front coupled with the excessive loss of tanks all combined to derail the American attack. The Americans soon became badly tangled and disoriented along their whole front and co-ordination of attacks quickly broke down. The British too became disorganised as they crossed the canal but they were able to reform promptly on a well-defined landmark as well as enjoying the respite granted through the capture of thousands of Germans along the bluffs, who had been cowed by the terrifying bombardment unleashed on them. The Americans on the other hand were tangled in wire and unfamiliar trenches while confronted by a vigilant and aggressive enemy.

Two positions of considerable strength anchored both ends of the unconquered portion of the outpost line. They were the villages of Vendhuille northeast of the Knoll and Bony southeast of Quennemont Farm. Both provided deadly enfilade against troops striking at either end of the outpost line. Incorporated into the main defensive system, Bony was gained only when the Germans withdrew to the Beaurevoir Line. Vendhuille was similarly abandoned. Throughout the operation Vendhuille was only prodded at by British troops offering limited support to the American left flank. It should have been attacked in force as a means of protecting the American flank. The logic for broadening the attack front to the IX Corps sector below Bellicourt was to stretch the German capacity to reinforce the tunnel sector. The same logic could and should have been applied to the other flank irrespective of the loss of confidence and perceived exhaustion of the III Corps. Fire and reinforcements from Vendhuille crippled the Americans on more than one occasion.

By far the most devastating decision to the Americans was that which denied them adequate artillery cover in the main attack for 29 September. A 1,000-yard advance against a position known to be laced with machine guns, over ground already strewn with the dead of previous attempts, in the hope of catching a barrage line set a further 200 yards beyond defied commonsense. As one American bitterly reflected, the barrage may as well have been set on Berlin for all the good it did them. Tanks were brought in as compensation for the lack of artillery cover but they proved an abject failure.

Except in a few isolated instances the Bellicourt Tunnel battle was a disastrous one for the Tank Corps. The fog caused difficulties with finding direction but the greater problem for the tanks – apart from the catastrophic self destruction in the old British minefield – was the expert placement of numerous anti-tank guns allocated to the German defence of the tunnel sector.

141

This area was the natural avenue of attack for the British and American armour and the Germans prepared well for it.

The most pervasive myth associated with the battle was whether the Americans failed to mop up. This was roundly believed to be the case by Australians from their commanding general down to the rank and file – despite it being a factor dismissed by the Australian official historian. The Americans too have entered into this myth as well by claiming that the Germans kept popping up from secret tunnels in their rear after they had passed over the enemy trenches. In fact there was little of this. Adherence to such a story possibly made the American failure more palatable.

Certainly American inexperience meant that their 'mopping up' technique was possibly deficient in some instances. In the main though the problems lay elsewhere. The fog caused sections of Germans to be missed in both the initial and secondary phases of the operation by the few groups of doughboys who got through the outpost and Hindenburg lines. Thereafter German reinforcements opposing the 27th Division were pushed forwards from the towns and trenches in the main line down the valleys to the threatened strongholds in the outpost line, while against the 30th Division they were brought up from the rear to bolster Le Catelet–Nauroy Line. The tunnel itself was not used as either an avenue or collection area for reinforcing troops.

Apart from the lack of artillery cover, the factor that compromised the American advance most was the strength and purpose in which the outpost line was defended by the Germans across the 27th Division front, at Bony and Le Catelet–Nauroy Line in the 30th Division sector. American units were shattered and disorganised by the heavy fire that was directed against them in these areas. The inexperience of the Americans and the losses amongst their front-line officers both further contributed to their eventual, and it must be said, rapid disorganisation.

In contrast to the inexperience of the Americans the diggers performed with professional surety. Despite the disruption to their original battle plan they

142

adapted quickly to the situation confronting them and managed to stabilise the Australian–American Corps front. The stiff fighting that these seasoned troops then endured was testament to just how strong the German will and position were in this part of the field. It was hardly surprising that troops new to the front and lacking in experience did not crack open the German line. It took a further two days' fighting by seasoned troops to loosen the German grip on this part of the line.

The exception to the difficulties encountered along the tunnel mound was the stunning success of the British 46th Division. There can be no doubt that the high command did not really expect the North Midland Division to gain the success it did. It was an exercise in hope and one that proved unexpectedly decisive. The carriage of the canal line south of Bellicourt, in tandem with Captain Wark's intrepid performance, dislodged the German line allowing the opportunity eventually to turn the German left opposite Monash's corps, belatedly gaining the Green Line and bringing the advance up to the Beaurevoir Line for the next phase of the Fourth Army operation.

Appendix – Order of Battle

Fourth Army (Lieutenant-General Henry S. Rawlinson)
29 September 1918

III Corps (Lieutenant-General Sir R. H. K. Butler)

12th Division (Major-General H. W. Higginson)
18th Division (Major-General R. P. Lee)

Artillery

RAF: 35th Squadron
Royal Engineers: 283rd A. T. Company

IX Corps (Lieutenant-General Sir. W. P. Braithwaite)

1st Division (Major-General E. P. Strickland)
6th Division (Major-General T. O. Marden)
32nd Division (Major-General T. S. Lambert)
46th Division (Major-General G. F. Boyd)

Artillery

RAF: 9th Squadron
3 Tank Brigade   (Brigadier-General J. Hardress-Lloyd)
      6th Tank Battalion (Whippets)
      5th Tank Battalion (Mark V)
      9th Tank Battalion (Mark V)

Royal Engineers: 216th, 221st, 567th A. T. Companies
    180th, 253rd, 254th, 256th (T) Companies
    No. 1 Special Company (Mortars)
    4th Siege Company

XIII Corps – Army Reserve – (Lieutenant-General Sir T. L. N. Morland)
25th Division (Major-General J. R. E. Charles)
50th Division (Major-General H. C. Jackson)
66th Division (Major-General H. K. Bethell)

Australian Corps (Lieutenant-General Sir J. Monash)
2nd Division (Major-General C. Rosenthal)
3rd Division (Major-General J. Gellibrand)
5th Division (Major-General Sir J. J. T. Hobbs)

Artillery
5 Cavalry Brigade (attached) (Brigadier-General N. W. Haig)
Australian Flying Corps: 3rd Squadron (also serving American II Corps)
5 Tank Brigade (Brigadier-General A. Courage)
    3rd Tank Battalion (Whippets)
    8th Tank Battalion (Mark V)
    13th Tank Battalion (Mark V and Mark V Star)
    16th Tank Battalion (Mark V and Mark V Star)
    17th Armoured Car Battalion
Royal Engineers: 146th, 238th A. T. Companies
    No. 2, Advance Section 353rd E and M Companies
    No. 4 Special Companies

No. 11 Pontoon Park

1st and 2nd Australian T Companies

American II Corps (Major-General G. W. Read)

27th Division (Major-General J. F. O'Ryan)

30th Division (Major-General E. M. Lewis)

4 Tank Brigade (Brigadier-General E. B. Hankey)

       1st Tank Battalion (Mark V and Mark V Star)

       4th Tank Battalion (Mark V and Mark V Star)

301st Tank Battalion (Mark V and Mark V Star)

Royal Engineers: 182nd (T) Company

       No. 1, Advance Section 353rd E and M Companies

       1st Siege Company

Cavalry Corps – GHQ Reserve (Lieutenant-General Sir C. T. McM. Kavanagh)

1st Cavalry Division (Major-General R. L. Mullens)

3rd Cavalry Division (Major-General A. E. W. Harman)

4 Guards Brigade

Household M. G. Brigade

RAF: 6th Squadron

Army Troops

5 Brigade, RAF (Brigadier-General L. E. O. Charlton)

15th Wing, RAF (Colonel J. Chamier)

       8th Squadron

       73rd Scout Squadron

22nd Wing (Lieutenant-Colonel P. A. E. Cairns)
>   23rd Squadron (Dolphin)
>   24th Squadron (SE5)
>   84th Squadron (SE5)
>   85th Squadron (SE5)
>   92nd Squadron (SE5)
>   46th Squadron (Camels)
>   80th Squadron (Camels)
>   208th Squadron (Camels)
>   20th Squadron (Bristol Fighter)
>   205th Squadron (De H 9)

Balloon Wing (Colonel F. F. M. Roxby)

Other Troops in GHQ Reserve

2nd Tank Battalion (5 Brigade)

>   Royal Engineers: 213th A. T. Company, 182nd (T) Company, 353rd E and M Companies (less advanced sections), D and Z Special Companies.

Notes

Introduction

1 Monash included the 17th and 32nd British Divisions as part of his calculation as each had been attached to the Australian Corps at various stages. John Monash, *The Australian Victories in France in 1918*, Melbourne, Lothian Book Publishing Company, 1923 [1920], p. 17.

2 Mitchell Yockelson, *Borrowed Soldiers: Americans under British Command, 1918*, Norman, OK, University of Oklahoma Press, 2008, pp. 70–71.

3 Yockelson, pp. 19–20.

4 Haig to Pershing, 14 June 1918, G-3, GHQ, AEF report 'Employment of American Divisions' in *United States Army in World War 1917– 1919: Training and Use of American Units with British and French*, vol. 3 (Washington, Historical Division: Department of the Army, 1948), pp.109–10.

5 For a discussion of this episode, see Dale Blair, ' "Diggers" and "Doughboys": Australian and American troop interaction on the Western Front, 1918.' *Australian War Memorial e-journal*, no. 35 (December 2001).

6 Monash, p. 242.

Chapter 1

1 Military Operations France and Belgium 1918, vol. V, Imperial War

Museum, p. 96.

2 *United States Army in the World War 1917–1919, Military Operations of the American Expeditionary Forces, Somme Offensive,* vol. 7 (hereafter cited as US-MO), Washington, Historical Division, Department of the Army, 1948, p. 325.

3 Imperial War Museum (IWM), Brigadier-General T. S. Lambert, 80/10/3, 'Notes on the Area East of Hindenburg Line. Captured German Defence Schemes etc', German Defence Scheme. St Quentin Sector of the Siegfried Line, see 5 (ii), Enemy's estimate of weak points.

4 John Buchan, *Nelson's History of the War: The Dawn,* vol. XXIII, London, Thomas Nelson and Sons, p. 169.

5 US-MO, p. 99.

6 Gregory Blaxland, *Amiens 1918,* Frederick Muller, London, 1968, pp. 221–2.

7 Blaxland, p. 230.

8 Monash, pp. 255–60. See Appendix I.

9 Liddell Hart Centre for Military Archives, King's College, London, Montgomery Massingherd collection, 7/26/2.

10 Monash, p. 277.

11 C. E. W. Bean, *Official History of Australia in the War of 1914–18: The AIF in France 1918,* vol. VI, Sydney, Angus & Robertson, 1942, p. 986, fn. 26.

12 Major-General Sir Archibald Montgomery, *The Story of the Fourth Army in the Battles of the Hundred Days, August 8th to November 11th 1918,* London, Hodder & Stoughton, 1919, p. 154.

13 AWM 38, 3DRL 606, Item 274A [1], Monash's battle plan as told to and recorded by C. E. W. Bean on night of 28 September 1918.

14 Peter Pederson, *Monash as Military Commander,* p. 284.

15 US-MO, p. 97, n. 1.

16 Major-General Sir Frederick Maurice (ed.), *The Life of General Lord Rawlinson of Trent: From His Journals and Letters,* London, Cassell, 1928,

pp. 239–40.

17 Bean, p. 947.

18 M. B. Keatinge, *War Book of the Third Pioneer Battalion*, Committee of the 3rd Pioneer Battalion, Battalion Associations, 1919 [reprint n.d. (early 1980s)], p. 135.

19 Pederson, p. 284.

20 AWM 38, 3DRL 606, Item 274A [1], Monash's battle plan as told to and recorded by C. E. W. Bean on night of 28 September 1918.

21 US-MO, p. 271.

22 US-MO, p. 273.

23 Dale Blair, 'Anti-British Sentiment in the Australian Imperial Force', *War & Society*, vol. 19, n. 1 (2001), pp. 71–92.

24 Bean, pp. 875–6. For a fuller account of the mutiny see Dale Blair, *Dinkum Diggers: An Australian Battalion at War*, Melbourne, Melbourne University Press, 2001, pp. 157–63.

25 IWM, O. G. Blows, 28th Bn, 7th Bde, AIF, 81/19/1 Con Shelf, 'War Diary', 26 September 1918.

26 Lance-Corporal Eric Russell, AWM, PR 87/96.

27 Geoffrey Serle, *Monash: A Biography*, Melbourne, Melbourne University Press, 1982, pp. 361–2.

28 Pederson, p. 285.

29 US War College, RG 120, 1017 Personal-Estimates of General Officers of the English Army <902>, p. 10. The author was Major Geo. S. Simmonds. He also described Monash as being 'not of pleasing personality' but 'an extremely able soldier of keen mentality'. He described Blamey, Monash's chief of staff , as 'efficient' but of 'average ability'.

30 Extracts from daily operation reports American II Corps, AWM 45, 48/1, Report, Headquarters 54th Infantry Brigade, AEF, France, 2 October 1918.

31 Gerald F. Jacobson, *History of the 107th Infantry, USA*, New York, 7th Regiment Armory, 1920, pp. 108, 122–3.

32 Military History Institute, Carlisle, WW1–200. 30th Division, Box 2. 'Over There For Uncle Sam: A Daily Diary of World War One', entry for 25 September 1918.

33 Military History Institute, Carlisle, WW1–200. 30th Division, Box 2. 'Over There For Uncle Sam: A Daily Diary of World War One', entry for 25 September 1918. For a discussion of treatment of German and Australian soldiers at the moment of surrender, see D. Blair, *No Quarter: Unlawful Killing and Surrender in the Australian War Experience, 1915–18*, ACT, Ginninderra Press, 2005.

34 Military History Institute, Carlisle, WW1–200. 30th Division, Box 2. 'Over There For Uncle Sam: A Daily Diary of World War One', entry for 25 September 1918.

35 AWM 4 Roll 35, 4th Battalion, 4 October 1918.

Chapter 2

1   Montgomery, p. 167.

2   Bean, p. 953; US-MO, pp. 301–2, 304.

3   US-MO, p. 246.

4   Monash, pp. 277–9.

5   AWM, MSS 196, 106th American Infantry Regiment, M Company History, 27 September 1918, p. 1.

6   US-MO, p. 271.

7   CM 1998.1 His 23rd and 106th Infantry NY Fld 8, p. 289.

8   Bean, p. 984.

9   US-MO, p. 304.

10 US-MO, p. 245.

11 US-MO, p. 303.

12 Bean, p. 984.

13 US-MO, p. 304.

14 Blaxland, p. 232.

15 AWM, MSS 196, 106th American Infantry Regiment, M Company History, 27 September 1918, p. 3.

16 Bean, p. 985.

17 Major-General John F. O'Ryan, *The Story of the 27th Division*, vol. I, New York, Wynkoop Hallenbeck Crawford, 1921, pp. 500–22.

18 O'Ryan, p. 285.

19 US-MO, pp. 303–5.

20 Bean, p. 985.

21 AWM 26, 481/3, Record of Operations, Tank Corps, p. 6.

22 US-MO, pp. 304–5.

23 Stephen Harris, *Duty, Honor, Privilege: New York's Silk Stocking Regiment and the Breaking of the Hindenburg Line*, Dulles, VA, Brassey, 2001, p. 219.

24 Bean, p. 985.

25 AWM 26, 481/3, Record of Operations, Tank Corps, pp. 4–6.

26 Bean, p. 984.

27 US-MO, p. 305.

28 US-MO, p. 305.

29 US-MO, p. 305.

30 US-MO, pp. 305–6.

31 US-MO p. 307.

32 Major-General Sir Arthur B. Scott and P. Middleton Brummell, *History of the 12th (Eastern) Division in the First World War*, London, Nisbet, 1923, p. 210.

33 R. S. H. Moody, *The Historical Records of The Buffs (East Kent Regiment) 3rd Foot, 1914–1919*, London, The Medici Society, 1922, pp. 378–9.

34 Bean, p. 986.

35 Jacobson, p. 109.

36 Claude G. Leland, *From Shell Hole to Chateau with Company I: Personal Recollections of a Line Officer of the 107th US Infantry, 27th Division, in France, 1918,* New York, New York National Guard, The Society of Ninth

Company Veterans, 7th Regiment, 1950, pp. 196–7.

37 Leland, p. 198.

38 AWM 45, 48/1, Report, Headquarters 54th Infantry Brigade, AEF, France, 2 October 1918.

39 US-MO, p. 307.

40 AWM 26, 484/9, Extracts from War Diary of HQ 138th Infantry Brigade, 5th Batallion Leicester Regiment, 29 September 1918, 4 p.m.

41 Maurice (ed.), p. 238.

42 Pederson, pp. 287–8.

43 US-MO, pp. 309–10; Pederson, p. 289; Monash, p. 273.

44 Leland, p. 198.

Chapter 3

1 Monash, p. 279.

2 IWM, 84/11/2. Major H. J. C. Marshall, Narrative/Journal VI.

3 IWM, 84/11/2. Major H. J. C. Marshall, Narrative/Journal VI.

4 AWM 26, 484/9, 46th Division, 137th Infantry Brigade Report.

5 AWM 26, 484/9, 46th Division, HQ RA.

6 IWM, 84/11/2. Major H. J. C. Marshall, Narrative/Journal VI.

7 IWM, Misc. Box 25, Item no. 442 T, 'Account of Capture of the Riqueval Bridge, Sept 1918', Letter to Director, IWM, late February 1978 from Private A. G. Shennan 'B' Company 1st North Staffordshire Regiment 46th North Midland Division; AWM 26, 484/9, 46th Division, 137th Infantry Brigade Report; H. C. B. Cook, *The North Staffordshire Regiment (Prince of Wales),* Famous Regiment's Series, London, Leo Cooper, 1970, p. 93.

8 IWM, 84/11/2. Major H. J. C. Marshall, Narrative/Journal VI.

9 Raymond E. Priestley, *Breaking The Hindenburg Line: The Story of the 46th (North Midland) Division,* London, T. Fisher Unwin, 1919, pp. 55–6.

10 Anon. (A Committee of Officers who served with the Battalion), *The War*

History of the Sixth Battalion The South Staffordshire Regiment (T. F.), London, William Heinemann, 1924, pp. 214–17.

11 Capt W. C. C. Weelman, *History of 1/8th Battalion Sherwood Foresters 1914–1919*, Nottingham, Thos Forman & Sons, 1920, p. 270.

12 IWM, 84/11/2. Major H. J. C. Marshall, Narrative/Journal VI.

13 Weelman, p. 266.

14 AWM 26, 484/9, 46th Division, 137th Infantry Brigade Report.

15 IWM, 80/10/4, Brigadier-General T. S. Lambert, 46th Division Operation 'C' Instruction no. 6, 27 September 1918.

16 AWM 26, 484/9, 46th Division, 138th Infantry Brigade Report, 1 October 1918.

17 AWM 26, 484/9, 46th Division, 138th Infantry Brigade Report, 1 October 1918.

18 Blaxland, p. 236.

19 H. Essame, *The Battle for Europe 1918*, London, B. T. Batsford, 1972, p. 188.

20 IWM, S. E. Butler, 86/2/1, typed manuscript 'Peppard, The Hindenburg Line and Return', p. 39.

21 IWM, J. A. Whitehead, 79/23/1, handwritten memoirs September 1939 'Four Years Memories' rewritten 1959.

Chapter 4

1 AWM 38, "The Breaking of the Hindenburg Line: The Final Attack of the 5th Division, AIF, in France" by Captain T. C. Barbour, 30th Battalion, p. 1.

2 Military History Institute, Carlisle, Dept of the Army: WW1 Research Project: Army Service Experiences Questionnaire (1914–1921), 1 December 1978,

Box 1, 30th Division, Private Luther J. Morris, Co. 'F', 105th Engineer, WW1–1625.

3 Bean, pp. 986–7.

4 Military History Institute, Carlisle, Dept of the Army: WW1 Research Project: Army Service Experiences Questionnaire (1914–1921), 1 December 1978, Box 1, 30th Division, Private George L. Jemerson, 119th Infantry Regiment, WW1–744.

5 Bean, fn. 31, p. 987.

6 AWM 26, 481/3. HQ Tank Corps, Report on Bellicourt Operations, Lieutenant-Colonel H. H. Johnson, 1st Tank Battalion.

7 US-MO, p.328.

8 AWM 26, 481/3. HQ Tank Corps, Report on Bellicourt Operations, Lieutenant-Colonel H. H. Johnson, 1st Tank Battalion.

9 Bean, fn. 46, p. 992.

10 AWM 4, Headquarters, 1st Australian Divisional Artillery, Roll 199, Report from liaison officer with the 3rd Battalion, 120th Regiment, American 30th Division, 29–30 September, dated 13 October 1918.

11 Bean, p. 987. See footnotes.

12 AWM 4, Headquarters, 1st Australian Divisional Artillery, Report from liaison officer with the 3rd Battalion, 120th Regiment, American 30th Division, 29–30 September, Roll 199.

13 Bean, p. 992.

14 Bean, p. 992.

15 Captain B. H. Liddell Hart, *The Tanks: The History of the Royal Tank Regiment and Its Predecessors Heavy Branch Machine Gun Corps, 1914–45*, vol. I, London, Cassell, 1959, p. 190.

16 Bean, pp. 987–8.

17 Bean, p. 988.

18 Collection RG 120, 30th Division, G. 3 Field messages, 28–29 September 1918, Box 12055, Telephone message to General Tyson at 12.50 NAA, College Park, Md ; To General Tyson by General Lewis: 12.55; Bean, p. 992.

19 Bean, fn. 47, p. 993.

20 Bean, p. 994.

21 Collection RG 120, 30th Division, Observations of battlefield of September 29 <230–33.9> Box 12058.

22 Collection RG 120, 30th Division, G. 3 Field messages, 28–29 September 1918, Box 12055, To General Tyson by General Lewis: 12.55.

23 AWM 3DRL 6850, Papers of Lieutenant-General Sir Iven Gifford Mackay, Box 1, Item 6, Diary 30 September 1918.

24 Collection RG 120, 30th Division, Observations of battlefield of 29 September <230–33.9> Box 12058.

25 Training Bulletin, 'Program of training for week, Sept 16–21 inclusive', Collection RG 120, Box 12059 <230–504>.

26 Yves Fohlen, *With Guts and Bayonets: Diggers and Doughboys on the Hindenburg Line, 1918*, Loftus, NSW, Publishing Services, 2001, p. 79.

27 University of Leeds, E. C. P. Thomas, 32nd Battalion, Staff Officer 9 Brigade HQ, typed recollections 27 January 1988, p. 25.

28 Lieutenant-General H. Sloan, *The Purple and Gold: A History of the 30th Battalion*, Sydney, [?publisher], 1938 [reprint], p. 346.

29 AWM 38, 'The Breaking of the Hindenburg Line: The Final Attack of the 5th Division, AIF, in France' by Captain T. C. Barbour, 30th Battalion, p. 2.

Chapter 5

1 Henry Berry, *Make The Kaiser Dance*, New York, Doubleday, 1978, p. 216.

2 Jacobson, p. 377.

3 Berry, pp. 216–18.

4 Bean, p. 989.

5 Leeds University Liddle Collection, Corporal F. S. Duffy, K Company, 107th Infantry Regiment, typed manuscript 'Ed and I went up on the Hill

and watched the War': The World War One Diary of Corporal Francis Joseph Duffy, Diary, 29 September 1918, p. 142.

6 J. F. Oakleaf, Notes on the Operations of the 108th Infantry Overseas, printed for the first reunion of Company "I" 108th Infantry, USA, 1921. Online edition at WW1 Memoirs and Remembrances (http://net.lib.byu. edu/estu/wwi/memoir/oakleaf/108th.htm), p. 13.

7 Bean, p. 992.

8 Oakleaf, p. 13.

9 US-MO, pp. 310–11.

10 US-MO, p. 314.

11 Oakleaf, p. 13.

12 Jacobson, p. 375.

13 Jacobson, pp. 377–8.

14 Leland, pp. 201–2.

15 Jacobson, p. 377.

16 Jacobson, p. 306.

17 Berry, p. 217.

18 AWM 45, 48/1, 3rd Batallion HQ, 107th US Infantry, from CO 3rd Batallion to CO HQ 27th Division. Report of operations, 29 September 1918; Bean, p. 991; US-MO, p. 314.

19 F. C. Green, *The Fortieth: A Record of the 40th Battalion, AIF.,* Hobart, John Vail, Government Printer, 1922 [reprint], p. 193.

20 Leland, pp. 205–6.

21 Leland, pp. 205–6. He had sent the German rearward with a wounded American he had found lying under a hedge.

22 US-MO, p. 314.

23 G. H. F. Nichols, *The 18th Division in the First World War*, London, William Blackwood & Sons, 1922, pp. 418–19.

24 Nichols, p. 423.

25 AWM 224, MSS 196, '106th American Inf. Regiment, M Company',

pp. 5–6.

26 Bean, p. 990; US-MO, p. 318.

27 Bean, fn. 45, p. 992.

28 US-MO, p. 316.

29 US-MO, pp. 310–11.

30 Jacobson, 'Notice to report of 1st Lieutenant W. O. Pasefield, 11th Australian Field Artillery Brigade in regard to operations of the 27th Division, 29 September 1918, pp. 122–3; Edward M. Coffman, *The War To End All Wars: The American Military Experience in World War 1*, Oxford, Oxford University Press, 1968, p. 296.

31 Jacobson, pp. 122–3.

32 US-MO, p. 316.

33 Harris, p. 267.

34 Nichols, pp. 419–24.

35 Lieutenant-Colonel Sir Albert G. Stern, *Tanks, 1914–1918: The Log-book of a Pioneer*, Hodder and Stoughton, London, 1919, p. 234.

36 US-MO, p. 314.

37 AWM 26, 481/3, HQ Tank Corps, Report on Bellicourt operations, 29 September 1918.

38 Bean, fn. 41, p. 960.

39 US-MO, p. 311.

40 Leeds University Liddle Collection, Major T. L. Leigh-Mallory, RFC/RAF Air 189, transcript, History of Tank and Aeroplane Co-operation, p. 19.

41 US-MO, p. 313; IWM Colonel F. J. Rice, 78/29/1, Diary 29 September 1918; Nichols, p. 424.

42 Bean, p. 991.

43 US-MO, p. 316.

44 Brand to O'Ryan, 1 October 1918, AWM 3DRL 2730.

45 Fohlen, p. 79.

46 James W. Rainey, 'Ambivalent Warfare: The Tactical Doctrine of the AEF in World War One', Parameters, vol. 13, no. 3 (September 1983), passim; James W. Rainey, 'The Questionable Training of the AEF in World War One', Parameters, vol. 22 (Winter 1992–3), passim. Not all have agreed that the Pershing doctrine was ambiguous or misplaced. Frederick Palmer believed, given the turnaround of fortunes that followed the blunting of the Kaiser's March offensive in 1918, that Pershing's advocacy of open warfare marked him as 'a true prophet' to those under his command (Frederick Palmer, America in France: The Story of the Making of an Army, London, John Murray, 1919, p. 229). Of course, Palmer's friendship with Pershing may have influenced his assessment.

47 Collection RG 120, 1003.1, Employment of Troops, Agreement and program of training concerning American Troops with British <692>, National Archives, College Park, Maryland.

48 Department of the Army, Office of Military History; *The United States Army in World War 1917–1919*, 17 vols, Training and Use of American Units with British and French, vol. 3 (1948), p.121, cited in Fred Davis Baldwin, 'The American Enlisted Man in World War One', Princeton, Princeton University, NJ, PhD, 1964.

49 Bean, p. 951.

Chapter 6

1 Bean, p. 958.

2 Keatinge, p. 140.

3 Bean, p. 959; Green, pp. 192–3.

4 Bede Nairn and Geoffrey Serle (eds), *Australian Dictionary of Biography*, vol. 9: 1891–1939, Gil-Las, Carlton, Victoria, Melbourne University Press, 1983, p. 37.

5 AWM, 3 DRL 2379, Brigadier-General H. A. Goddard, 9th Infantry Brigade AIF, Diary, 29 September 1918, 1 of 14.

6   Bean, p. 959.

7   Green, p. 197.

8   Leland, pp. 206–7.

9   Green, p. 194. Leland referred to the officer as a captain but none of the company commanders in the 40th Battalion appears to have been so badly wounded on 29 September; Bean, pp. 961–2.

10 Berry, pp. 217–18.

11 Green, pp. 194–5.

12 Green, p. 195.

13 Scott & Brummell, pp. 379–80.

14 Anon., *The Thirty-Ninth: The History of the 39th Battalion, Australian Imperial Force,* Melbourne, G. W. Green & Sons, 1934, p. 235; Sargeant E. W. Billing had brought back similar information to the 40th Battalion. See Green, p. 196.

15 Anon., *The Forty-First: Being a Record of the 41st Battalion, AIF during the First World War 1914–18,* Compiled by Members of the Intelligence Staff, Battalion Associations, 1919 [reprint n.d. (early 1980s)], p. 132.

16 Bean, pp. 963–5.

17 Ross McMullin, *Pompey Elliott*, Melbourne, Scribe Publications, 2002, p. 492.

18 Bean, p. 964.

19 Bean, p. 996.

20 Captain C. Longmore, *'Eggs-A-Cook': The Story of the Forty-Fourth: War as the Digger Fought It,* Perth, WA, The Colortype Press, 1921 [reprint], p. 123.

21 Bean, fn. 38, p. 990.

22 AWM 25, Reports on Operations – Operation Orders and Instruction 2nd, 3rd, 13th, 15th and 17th Tank battalions, August-September, 1918.

23 Bean, p. 995.

24 Bean, p. 995.

25 Bean, pp. 965–7.

26 Bean, pp. 995–6.

27 Bean, pp. 965–7.

28 Longmore, p. 122.

29 IWM, Major H. J. C. Marshall, 84/11/2, Narrative/Journal VI, p. 145.

Chapter 7

1 US-MO, p. 320.

2 Bean, p. 969.

3 Corfield, pp. 183–4.

4 Bean, p. 970.

5 Bean, p. 996.

6 A. D. Ellis, *The Story of the Fifth Division*, London, Hodder & Stoughton, 1920, p. 370.

7 AWM 38, Narrative, 'The Battle of the Hindenburg Line – Bellicourt – Nauroy: The Part Taken by the 29th Battalion AIF from 29 September to 1 October, inclusive, 1918' by Captain C. A. M. Derham MC, CO 29th Battalion, p. 3; AWM 26, 563/1, Report of the 13th Australian Field Artillery Brigade's portion of the operation of 29 and 30 September; Bean, p. 971.

8 Sloan, pp. 344–5.

9 Ron Austin, *Black and Gold: The History of the 29th Battalion, 1915–18*, McCrae, Victoria, Slough Hat Publications, 1997, p. 156.

10 Bean, p. 972; Austin, p. 157.

11 Sloan, pp. 211–13; Ellis, p. 371; Bean, p. 972; Austin, p. 157; Bean, p. 996.

12 Bean, p. 972.

13 Bean, p. 996.

14 Ellis, pp. 406–7. See transcript of Victoria Cross citation which Wark was awarded for these actions; AWM 38, 'The Battle of the Hindenburg Line'

by Major-General E. Tivey, p. 2; Bean, p. 996.

15 King's College, Liddell Hart Centre for Military Archives, Charrington 1/8, letter to Major-General Tivey re 32nd Battalion attack, 5 September 1935; Captain P. F. Stewart, *The History of the XII Royal Lancers (Prince of Wales)*, London, Oxford University Press, 1950, p. 302.

16 Blaxland, p. 237.

17 IWM, Major H. J. C. Marshall, 84/11/2, Narrative, Journal VI; A company of the Fort Garry Horse, a Canadian cavalry regiment, had won great plaudits for a gallant charge made at Cambrai on 20 November 1917. It is unclear from the narrative when exactly this incident occurred. It may have been a few days later when the cavalry was transferred to IX Corps control.

18 AWM 38, 'The Battle of the Hindenburg Line' by Major-General E. Tivey, p. 4.

Chapter 8

1 AWM 26, 530/3, Australian 3rd Division, General Staff, Part I, 10th Brigade to Colonel Jess, General McNicoll, 11.50 a.m.

2 AWM 26, 530/3, Australian 3rd Division, General Staff, Part I, Colonel Jess to GOC 10th Brigade. Outwards. 12.25 p.m.

3 AWM 26, 530/3, Australian 3rd Division, General Staff, Part I, 12.40 p.m. Italics added.

4 AWM 26, 530/3, Australian 3rd Division, General Staff, Part I, Colonel Jess to BM 9th Brigade, Outwards, 12.33 p.m.

5 AWM 26, 530/3, Australian 3rd Division, General Staff, Part I, Colonel Jess to General Cannan, Outwards, 12.50 p.m.

6 AWM 26, 530/3, Australian 3rd Division, General Staff, Part I, Colonel Jess to General Cannan, Outwards, 12.50 p.m.

7 AWM 26, 530/3, Australian 3rd Division, General Staff, Part I, GOC to General Blamey, Outwards, 1.10 p.m.

8 AWM 45, 48/1, 2nd Army Corps: record of messages received 27 September–10 October 1918. Date 9.30.18. Message: Col. Boswell timed 2.24 p.m.

9 Longmore, p. 122.

10 AWM 26, 530/3, General Blamey to Captain Dunbar, Phone, Inwards, 1.25 p.m., 29 September 1918.

11 AWM 26, 530/3, Colonel Jess to GOC 10th Brigad,. Outwards, 1.27 p.m.

12 Leland, p. 208.

13 Green, p. 198; Leland, p. 208.

14 Bean, p. 978

15 Eric Fairey, *The Story and Official History of the 38th Battalion, AIF.,* Bendigo, Victoria, Bendigo Advertiser and the Cambridge Press, 1920 [reprint], pp. 78–9; AWM 38, 3DRL 606, Item 274, 'Over The Top' with C Company of 38th Battalion, by CSM Rupert John Buckland, p. 4, also 'Operation by C Company 38th Battalion, AIF, 29 September 1918 near Gillemont Farm' by Captain C. H. Peters, pp. 1–3; Bean, p. 979.

16 AWM 26, 530/3, Australian 3rd Division, General Staff, Part I, G2 to General Gellibrand, Phone, 4 p.m.; G2 to General McNicoll, Phone, 4.12 p.m.; McNicoll to Jess, Phone, Inwards, 4.25 p.m.

17 Bean, p. 980; Vivian Brahms, *The Spirit of the Forty-Second: Narrative of the 42nd Battalion, 11th Infantry Brigade, 3rd Division, Australian Imperial Forces, during the First World War, 1914–1918*, Brisbane, W. R. Smith and Paterson, 1938, p. 115.

18 Bean, pp. 995–6.

19 Bean, p. 996.

20 Bean, p. 996.

21 Bean, pp. 981–2.

22 Bean, p. 997.

23 AWM 26, 530/3, Australian 3rd Division, General Staff, Part I, General

Gellibrand to Corps (Captain Roydhouse) Outwards, 5.45 p.m.

24 Bean, p. 997.

25 AWM 26, 530/3, Australian 3rd Division, General Staff, Part I, General Blamey to Colonel Jess, Phone, Inwards, 7.11 p.m. Monash's and Gellibrand's conversation timed at 7.22 p.m.

Chapter 9

1 Bean, p. 998.

2 Bean, p. 1006.

3 Bean, pp. 998–99.

4 Bean, pp. 999–1000.

5 Bean, p. 1000; see AWM 26, 530/3, Australian 3rd Division, General Staff, Part I for detailed discussions within various communications about the planning of the attack.

6 Maurice, pp. 68–70.

7 Bean, p. 1005.

8 Nichols, pp. 425–7.

9 Scott & Brummell, p. 212.

10 Green, pp. 198–9.

11 N.G. McNicol, *The History of the Thirty Seventh Battalion, AIF*, Melbourne, Modern Printing Company, 1936, p. 256.

12 Fairey, p. 78.

13 Bean, p. 1005.

14 Private V. G. Schwinghammer, 42nd Battalion, AWM, 2DRL 234.

15 Bean, p. 1001.

16 Brahms, p. 116.

17 Bean, p. 1004.

18 Captain E. J. Colliver and Lieutenant B. H. Richardson, *The Forty-Third: The Story and Official History of the 43rd Battalion, AIF*, Adelaide, Rigby, 1920, p. 231.

19 Bean, pp. 100–2. See fn. 67.

20 Bean, p. 1002.

21 Bean, pp. 1003, 1006.

22 AWM 26, 571/4, Part 2, Final Offensive 25 September–2 October, 14th Australian Infantry Brigade, Report, Lieutenant-Colonel Commanding 53rd Battalion, AIF.

23 Bean, p. 1003.

24 Bean, pp. 1006–7.

25 Bean, p. 1005.

26 Bean, p. 1007.

27 Bean, pp. 1007–8.

28 Bean, p. 1008.

29 Bean, pp. 1008–9.

30 Pederson, p. 290.

31 Pederson, p. 288.

Chapter 10

1 Bean, p. 1009.

2 Pederson, p. 291; Bean, p. 1009.

3 Monash, pp. 290–1.

4 IWM, Colonel F. J. Rice, 78/29/1, Diary entries September/October 1918.

5 Bean, p. 1013.

6 McNicol, p. 256.

7 Green, pp. 199–200.

8 McMullin, p. 493.

9 AWM 38, 'The Breaking of the Hindenburg Line: The final attack of the 5th Division, AIF, in France' by Captain T. C. Barbour, 30th Battalion, p. 4; Sloan, pp. 348–50.

10 Leeds University Liddle Collection, G. V. Rose, typed diary/memoir, 1

October 1918, pp. 142–3.

11 Sloan, pp. 350–1.

12 AWM 38, 'The Breaking of the Hindenburg Line: The final attack of the 5th Division, AIF, in France' by Captain T. C. Barbour, 30th Battalion, p. 5.

13 Leeds University Liddle Collection, G. V. Rose, typed diary/memoir, 1 October 1918, p. 144.

14 Fohlen, pp. 76–8.

15 Ellis, p. 380.

Conclusion

1 O'Ryan, p. 292.

Bibliography

Primary Sources
Australian War Memorial
AWM 4 AIF unit war diaries

AWM 26 Operations files

AWM 38 Bean, C. E. W., papers

AWM 45 Copies of British war diaries and other records

AWM 224 MSS 196, '106th American Infantry Regiment, M Company'

Military History Institute, Carlisle
Dept of the Army: WW1 Research Project: Army Service Experiences
  Questionnaire (1914–1921)

National Archives, College Park, Maryland
Collection RG 120

Official Sources
Military Operations France and Belgium 1918, vol. V

*United States Army in the World War 1917–1919, Military Operations of the American
  Expeditionary Forces, Somme Offensive,* vol. 7, Washington, DC, Historical
  Division, Department of the Army, 1948

Private collections (various)
Australian War Memorial (AWM)
Imperial War Museum (IWM)
King's College, Liddell Hart Centre
Leeds University Liddle Collection

Secondary Sources
Books, articles and theses

Anon. (A Committee of Officers who served with the Battalion), *The War History of the Sixth Battalion The South Staffordshire Regiment (T. F.)*, London, William Heinemann, 1924

Anon., *The Forty-First: Being a Record of the 41st Battalion, AIF during the First World War 1914–18*, Compiled by Members of the Intelligence Staff, Battalion Associations, 1919 [reprint n.d. (early 1980s)]

Anon., *The Thirty-Ninth: The History of the 39th Battalion, Australian Imperial Force*, Melbourne, G. W. Green & Sons, 1934

Austin, Ron, *Black and Gold: The History of the 29th Battalion, 1915–18*, McCrae, Victoria, Slouch Hat Publications, 1997

Baldwin, Fred Davis, 'The American Enlisted Man in World War One', Princeton, NJ, Princeton University, PhD, 1964

Bean, C. E. W., *Official History of Australia in the War of 1914–18: The AIF in France 1918*, vol. VI, Sydney, Angus & Robertson, 1942

Berry, Henry, *Make the Kaiser Dance*, New York, Doubleday, 1978

Blair, Dale, 'Anti-British Sentiment in the Australian Imperial Force', *War & Society*, vol. 19, no. 1 (2001)

Blair, Dale, '"Diggers" and "Doughboys": Australian and American troop interaction on the Western Front, 1918.' *Australian War Memorial* e-journal, no. 35 (December 2001)

Blair, Dale, *Dinkum Diggers: An Australian Battalion at War*, Melbourne, Melbourne University Press, 2001

Blair, Dale, *No Quarter: Unlawful Killing and Surrender in the Australian War Experience, 1915–18*, ACT, Ginninderra Press, 2005

Blaxland, Gregory, *Amiens 1918*, London, Frederick Muller, 1968

Brahms, Vivian, *The Spirit of the Forty-Second: Narrative of the 42nd Battalion, 11th Infantry Brigade, 3rd Division, Australian Imperial Forces, during the First World War, 1914–1918*, Brisbane, W. R. Smith and Paterson, 1938

Buchan, John, *Nelson's History of the War: The Dawn*, vol. XXIII, London, Thomas Nelson and Sons

Coffman, Edward M., *The War To End All Wars: The American Military Experience in World War 1*, Oxford, Oxford University Press, 1968

Colliver, Captain E. and Richardson, Lieutenant B. H., *The Forty-Third: The Story and Official History of the 43rd Battalion, AIF*, Adelaide, Rigby, 1920

Cook, H. C. B., *The North Staffordshire Regiment (Prince of Wales)*, Famous Regiments Series, London, Leo Cooper, 1970

Corfield, Robin S., *Hold Hard, Cobbers: The Story of the 57th and 60th and 57/60th Australian Infantry Battalions 1912–1930*, Glenhuntly, Victoria, 57/60th Battalion (AIF) Association, 1992

Ellis, A. D., *The Story of the Fifth Division*, London, Hodder & Stoughton, 1920

Essame, H, *The Battle for Europe 1918*, London, B. T. Batsford, 1972

Fairey, Eric, *The Story and Official History of the 38th Battalion, AIF,* Bendigo, Victoria, Bendigo Advertiser and the Cambridge Press, 1920

Fohlen, Yves, *With Guts and Bayonets: Diggers and Doughboys on the Hindenburg Line, 1918*, Loftus, NSW, Publishing Services, 2001

Green, F. C., *The Fortieth: A Record of the 40th Battalion, AIF*, Hobart, John Vail, Government Printer, 1922 [reprint]

Harris, Stephen L., *Duty, Honor, Privilege: New York's Silk Stocking Regiment and the Breaking of the Hindenburg Line*, Dulles, VA, Brassey, 2001

Jacobson, Gerald F., *History of the 107th Infantry, USA*, New York City, 7th Regiment Armory, 1920

Keatinge, M. B., *War Book of the Third Pioneer Battalion*, Committee of the 3rd Pioneer Battalion, Battalion Associations, 1919 [reprint n.d. (early 1980s)]

Leland, Claude G., *From Shell Hole to Chateau With Company I: Personal Recollections of a Line Officer of the 107th US Infantry, 27th Division, in France, 1918*, New York, New York National Guard, The Society of Ninth Company Veterans, 7th Regiment, 1950

Liddell Hart, Captain B. H., *The Tanks: The History of the Royal Tank Regiment and its Predecessors Heavy Branch Machine Gun Corps, 1914–45*, vol. I, London, Cassell, 1959

Longmore, Captain C., *'Eggs-A-Cook': The Story of the Forty-Fourth: War as the Digger Fought It*, Perth, WA, The Colourtype Press

McMullin, Ross, *Pompey Elliott*, Melbourne, Scribe Publications, 2002

McNicol, N. G., *The History of the Thirty-Seventh Battalion, AIF*, Melbourne, Modern Printing Company, 1936

Maurice, Major F., *The History of the 13th Tank Battalion*, London, Andrew Melrose, 1920

Maurice, Major-General Sir Frederick (ed.), *The Life of General Lord Rawlinson of Trent: From His Journals and Letters*, London, Cassell, 1928

Monash, John, *The Australian Victories in France in 1918*, Melbourne, Lothian Book Publishing Company, 1920 (1923 edition)

Montgomery, Major-General Sir Archibald, *The Story of the Fourth Army in the Battles of the Hundred Days, August 8th to November 11th 1918*, London, Hodder & Stoughton, 1919

Moody, R. S. H., *The Historical Records of The Buffs (East Kent Regiment) 3rd Foot, 1914–1919*, London, The Medici Society, 1922

Nairn, Bede and Serle, Geoffrey (eds), *Australian Dictionary of Biography*, vol. 9: 1891–1939, Gil-Las, Carlton, Victoria, Melbourne University Press, 1983

Nichols, G. H. F., *The 18th Division in the First World War*, London, William Blackwood & Sons, 1922

Oakleaf, J. F., *Notes on the Operations of the 108th Infantry Overseas*, printed for the first reunion of Company 'I' 108th Infantry, USA, 1921. Online edition at WW1 Memoirs and Remembrances (http://net.lib.byu.edu/estu/wwi/memoir/oakleaf/108th.htm)

O'Ryan, Major-General John F., *The Story of the 27th Division*, vol. I, New York, Wynkoop Hallenbeck Crawford, 1921

Palmer, Frederick, *America in France: The Story of the Making of an Army*, London, John Murray, 1919

Pederson, Peter, *Monash as Military Commander*, Melbourne, Melbourne University Press, 1985

Priestley, Raymond E., *Breaking The Hindenburg Line: The Story of the 46th (North Midland) Division*, London, T. Fisher Unwin, 1919

Rainey, James W., 'Ambivalent Warfare: The Tactical Doctrine of the AEF in World War One', *Parameters*, vol. 13, no. 3 (September 1983)

Rainey, James W., 'The Questionable Training of the AEF in World War One', *Parameters*, vol. 22 (Winter 1992–3)

Scott, Major-General Sir Arthur B. and Brummell, P. Middleton, *History of the 12th (Eastern) Division in the First World War*, London, Nisbet, 1923

Serle, Geoffrey, *Monash: A Biography*, Melbourne, Melbourne University Press, 1982

Sloan, Lieutenant-Colonel H., *The Purple and Gold: A History of the 30th Battalion*, Sydney, Halstead Press, 1938 [reprint]

Stern, Lieutenant-Colonel Sir Albert G., *Tanks, 1914–1918: The Log-book of a Pioneer*, London, Hodder and Stoughton, 1919

Stewart, Captain P. F., *The History of the XII Royal Lancers (Prince of Wales)*, London, Oxford University Press, 1950

Weelman, Captain W. C. C., *History of 1/8th Battalion Sherwood Foresters 1914–1919*, Nottingham, Thos Forman & Sons, 1920

Yockelson, Mitchell, *Borrowed Soldiers: Americans under British Command, 1918*, Norman, OK, University of Oklahoma Press, 2008

Index